Woodturning

Woodturning

Klaus Pracht

B.T. Batsford Ltd, London

Further reading

J. Bairstow, *Practical and decorative woodworking joints*, B.T. Batsford Ltd

Michael Bennet, *Refinishing antique furniture*, Dryad Press Ltd

Peter Child, *The craftsman woodturner*, Bell & Hyman Ltd

D. Hawkins, *Technique of wood surface decoration*, B.T. Batsford Ltd

D. Johnston, *Wood handbook for craftsmen*, B.T. Batsford Ltd

F. Pain, *The practical woodturner*, Bell & Hyman Ltd

Roland Seale, *Practical designs for woodturning*, Bell & Hyman Ltd

Gordon Stokes, *Modern woodturning*, Bell & Hyman Ltd

John Trussell, *Making furniture*, Dryad Press Ltd

John Trussell, *Working in wood: making boxes and small chests*, Dryad Press Ltd

© Rudolf Müller GmbH, Köln, 1986
English translation © Dryad Press Ltd, 1988

First published in German by Rudolf Müller GmbH, 1987
English language edition first published in 1988 by Dryad Press Ltd
Reprinted in 1991, 1993

Library of Congress Cataloguing in Publication Data

Pracht, Klaus.
  Woodturning.

  Translation of: Drechseln.
  Translated from the German.
  Bibliography: p.
  Includes index.
  1. Turning.   2. Woodwork.   I. Title

TT201.P7513 1988   684'.08   88–22909
ISBN 0–486–25887–4 (pbk.)

Printed and bound in Great Britain

Introduction

Woodturning reached its prime in the Middle Ages. Its greatest exponents were artists such as Leonardo da Vinci and the German sculptor and woodcarver, Veit Stoss, and Guilds set strict standards which controlled both the training and practice of the trade. Much later, industrialisation led to the decline of the traditional system and in the appreciation of crafts. The market became inundated with mass produced goods, including everything that had until then been produced by woodturning. This development meant that the craft of woodturning was driven almost to extinction. Turned wood was more or less disdained; workshops disappeared from towns and only a few craftsmen remained in villages.

Although interest in woodturning has never entirely disappeared, it has not readily adapted itself to modern times. The scope of woodturning can be extended beyond the production of small objects. It is possible for it to be used to give furniture and household articles new forms and new values. But professional turners still suffer difficulties because of the need to compete against mechanised production. They are forced to compete with industrial output, and so often have to produce much in series and at low prices. As a result, it is only very rarely that they can pursue and develop their own design ideas. They have to use their spare time if they want to be at all creative in their profession.

On the other hand, woodturning as a hobby has become more popular as the amount of leisure time people have has increased. A new interest in the craft has been awakened, which is well-deserved, since it can provide thoroughly convincing answers to questions of design.

The technique of woodturning has remained the same since time immemorial. The lathe has hardly changed in principle for centuries. It was originally an Oriental development from the lathe worked with one hand. Today's instruments came via the pole lathe, which was worked with the feet and so left both hands free, to water and electrically-powered lathes.

Woodturning is a process by which a workpiece is rotated and a profile cut or scraped into it by a tool held up against it. The workpiece is either mounted between the spindle and the tailstock, or it is held at one end in a chuck. The tools used are mostly gouges and chisels, but drills and more specialised turning tools are also available. The wood is worked from coarse to fine in a series of stages: roughing, profiling, smoothing, sanding and finishing.

Designing a piece of work that is both modern and suitable for the material used is like walking a tightrope between technical possibilities and aesthetic aims. Special techniques enable us to overcome difficulties and explore new ideas. Mastering these techniques, however, while it liberates the turner, also sets limits which confine him. He will often feel a strong inclination to remain rigidly within the confines of habit. To break free from this, and to create products of artistic merit, it is necessary to be trained in free design. 'Design begins where functionalism stops' said Sir Edwin Lutyens. It is not sufficient for objects to fulfil their functions: they must also have a symbolic value. Design is an integral part of training and professional practice in any craft, including woodturning.

Decoration and symbolism have been ignored, and even condemned, by modern architecture. But a purely functional design is not enough to satisfy people's needs completely. If utensils, furniture and houses are to be used properly, they must mean something to the people who use them. The functionalism developed by Gropius and Mies van der Rohe, which completely banished decoration – that doctrine of pure functionalism that has so often been misinterpreted by following generations – began as a protest against the overflowing forms of art nouveau. As the basis of modern building it has an undisputed historical justification. It cannot be rejected on principle, but the inherent contradiction between functional and aesthetic necessities needs to be recognised and taken into account.

People from all social classes have a desire for identification and symbolic values in objects that extends beyond functionalism. An object that means nothing to its user has failed in its purpose. Meaning must be established so that it appeals to everyone, that is, using everyday pictures and signs. Decoration is food for the soul; it brings objects to life.

Venturi expressed it thus: 'Design has the task of helping to make a society what it should be'.

The heart must be appealed to just as much as the head. Intuition and inspiration need to complement a rational understanding of the world. Variety rather than of uniformity, ambiguity rather than of clarity: this appears to suit us better than calculatedly correct statements. Design must be oriented towards the ideal of a better future if it is not to lose a substantial part of itself.

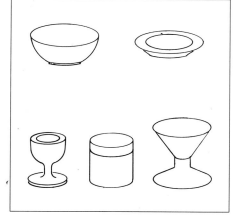

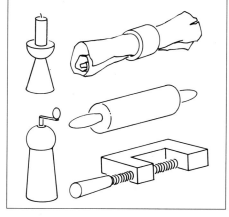

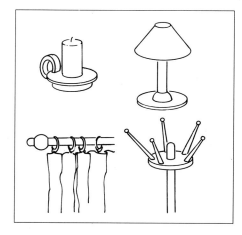

Contents

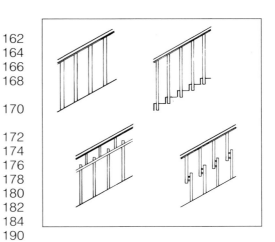

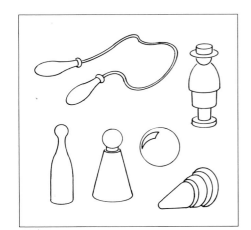

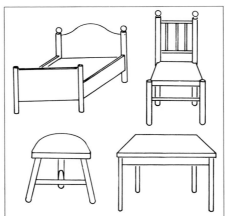

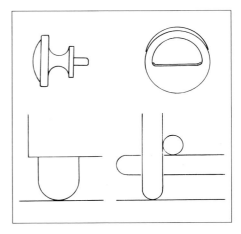

The earliest known turned objects were made by the Etruscans (c. 800 BC). Some ancient wooden dishes discovered during excavations to the north of Rome are evidence that woodturning was practised in antiquity. Many types of turned objects were in use at this time, including receptacles, dishes, legs and feet of furniture. Few works from Etruscan, Greek and Roman times have survived, however, as the wood used has usually rotted away in the course of time. The shapes and ornaments of turned wood have changed with the times and with styles. From the technical point of view, from early times variety was offered by the fact that wood could be turned in the side grain as well as in the end grain.

300 BC   Etruscan

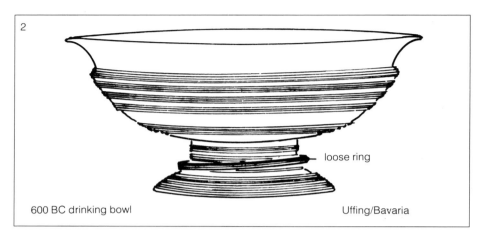

600 BC drinking bowl   loose ring   Uffing/Bavaria

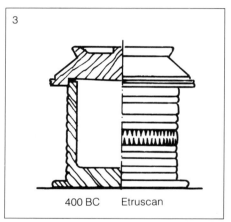

400 BC   Etruscan

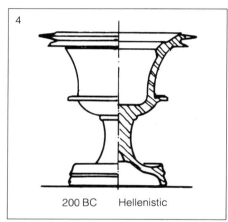

200 BC   Hellenistic

Fig 2 shows a wooden drinking bowl from about 600 BC. It was found almost intact in a tumulus near Uffing, Staffelsee in Bavaria. Apart from being perfectly shaped, the bowl has a loose ring around its base and is a masterpiece of the art of turning at that time. Detaching rings by cutting away from behind is still considered a special refinement in modern woodturning.

Figs 5, 6 and 7 show plain, straightforward Roman jars, decorated only by fine grooves and lines.

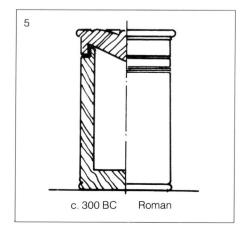

c. 300 BC   Roman

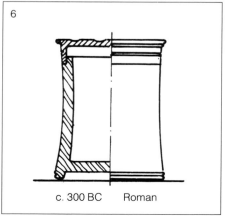

c. 300 BC   Roman

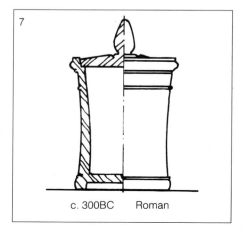

c. 300BC   Roman

Fig 8: A design similar to this slender American cottage chair is still produced today.

The North German baroque cupboard in Fig 9 is decorated with halved, twisted columns. The weighty feet are also turned.

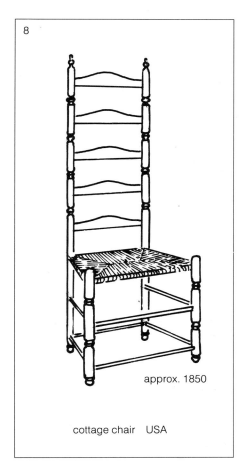

8

approx. 1850

cottage chair USA

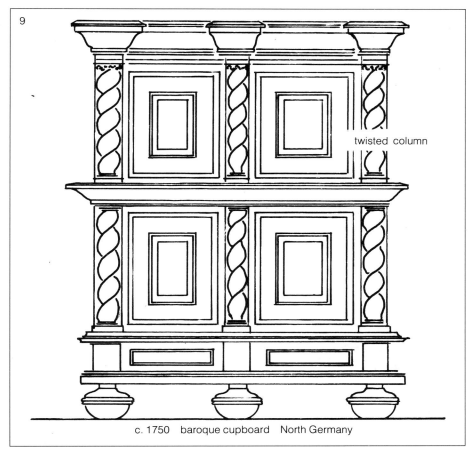

9

twisted column

c. 1750 baroque cupboard North Germany

The two pepper-mortars (Fig 11) were turned in about 1900 (Historic Museum, Hanover).

In Eastern countries such as Pakistan, India or Turkey, wooden containers, lattice-work and everyday objects are still turned on simple, hand-driven lathes.

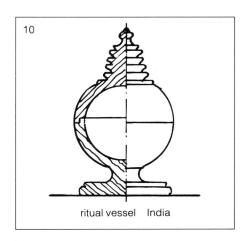

10

ritual vessel India

11

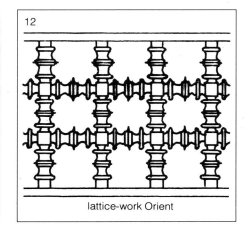

12

lattice-work Orient

The principle of woodturning dates back to prehistoric times when man, in order to make fire, used the palms of his hands to turn a wooden stick back and forth, with its pointed end pressed against a wooden block, thus causing friction and heat.

In the pole lathe, a string was wound round a workpiece and its ends secured to a pliable pole and a foot treadle. When the treadle was moved, the pole was pulled over by the string, which created enough tension to turn the workpiece back again.

1

1350 BC running drill   Egypt

4

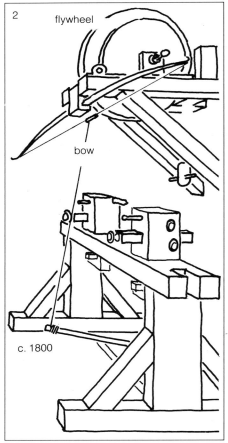

2   flywheel

bow

c. 1800

3

By about 3000 BC simple twist, or fiddle, drills had been invented. These were now driven by bows for increased speed. The principle of a simple lathe was discovered by winding the taut bowstring round a wooden rod that was inserted horizontally between two centres.

Later the twist drill was replaced by use of a cord which had to be moved back and forward by two assistants. This meant that the turner now had both hands free to hold his tools. By moving the centres to the left or right along the bed, he could work different lengths of wood.

In about 1500 Leonardo da Vinci invented the first lathe to use a crankshaft. For the first time wood was rotated in one direction only, towards the tool, which resulted in a continuous working process and a 50% better utilisation of time.

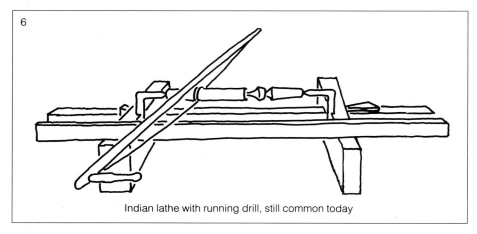

6

Indian lathe with running drill, still common today

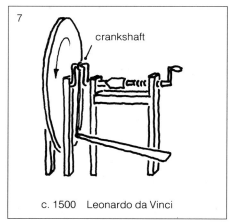

7   crankshaft

c. 1500   Leonardo da Vinci

Fig 8: The wooden lathe pictured here comes from Lower Saxony, dating from about 1900. It is now exhibited in the Historic Museum in Hanover.

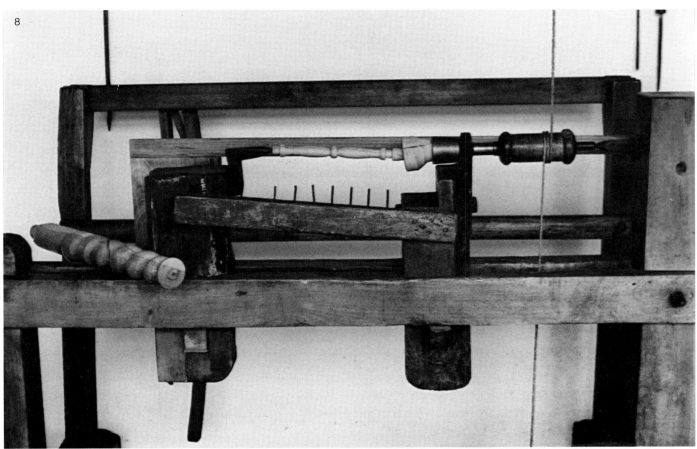

Figs 3 and 5 show a wooden lathe with a foot-treadle and a crankshaft. The tailstock is set in motion by a leather belt.

Many different types of lathe were later developed, driven either by manpower and flywheel or by water-power. Wooden treadle-driven lathes were worked by the turner himself, in a way similar to working a spinning-wheel, but the strength of one man alone was often not sufficient to turn larger objects.

The industrialisation and mechanisation of the nineteenth century transformed the woodturning lathe to one on which steel could be turned. These new lathes were made of cast iron, were driven by transmission belts or electric motors, were equipped with a tool support, and were basically the same as they are today.

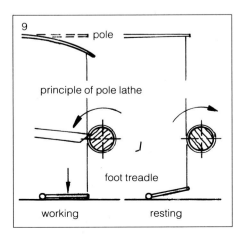

principle of pole lathe

foot treadle

working   resting

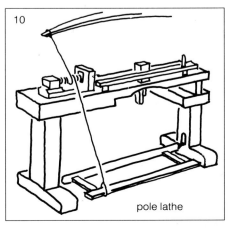

pole lathe

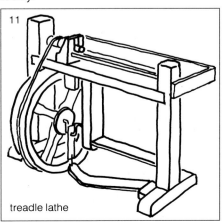

treadle lathe

1

The masterfully turned piece of work shown in Fig 1 was produced by Karl Pfander of Reutlingen.

The objects in Figs 2 and 3 were turned by Günther Kunst from Zetel and the ebony jars (Fig 4) by Karl Fecker from Lübeck. The circular constructions in Figs 5 and 6 were made by Peer Clahsen from Schoppheim.

2

3

4

The possibilities of finding new areas in which to apply woodturning are limited. Permanent experimentation is necessary if the craft is to remain living. The time in which we live is itself not harmonious, so it can hardly be accurately represented by objects designed purely according to such noble ideals as beauty, meaningfulness and charm.

As can be seen in our architecture, the things we produce today are marked by tension and contrast, or are even deliberately designed to disappoint our expectations. We love surprise and exaggeration; art no longer needs to be beautiful, and is often an expression of protest, weapon and struggle.

Because of the process by which it is worked, turned wood is round, and therefore harmonious. To a certain extent, this makes it a difficult medium in which to make statements relevant to our time.

Because of this, the design imposed after the process of turning is of great importance. After having been turned, objects can be finished in many different ways, some of which change the original shape completely. Turned objects can be split, for example, or cut up and the pieces put back in a different order.

Breaking the harmony of turned wood and, by doing so, increasing its artistic value is the idea behind radical changes made to enhance a statement.

Our society and our time should find expression in their products. Recourse to designs of earlier ages produces lifeless imitations and should therefore be avoided. However, looking back at antique models may provide guidelines for the judging of potential designs and their effect.

The use of turned wood in everyday life should be extended into practical areas. To produce small *objets d'art* is not enough – the theoretical studies on pages 216-7 show some results of experimental work.

Along with the choice of material and the surface treatment, deciding on the best shape is the most difficult part of design. It is better to design the shape to be turned vividly in three dimensions than in more abstract two-dimensional drawings. Sketches and drawings are good for trying out ideas, but ought also to be drawn three-dimensionally in perspective or in isometric diagrams.

The range of possible basic profile shapes is limited. Apart from rounded beads and hollows, there are V-cuts and squared shoulders. The proportions can be chosen either to harmonise or to create tension. The dimensions must be given particular consideration. This is often a question of scale. A perfectly-shaped door knob, designed to be gripped by the hand, does not easily lend itself to being enlarged to the size of a lampstand.

The turner's materials include ivory, horn, amber, plastics and some types of metal as well as the more common wood. The wood used by the turner varies in origin and in structure. There are hard and soft varieties, heartwood and sapwood, wood with open or closed pores, wood of light and dark colours, or with calm or lively grain. All these qualities must be considered as a starting-point for design.

A turner should do justice to his materials as well as to the technical possibilities. The cut of the wood and the way it is glued together are part of the design, but even more so are the decisions as to which way the grain should run and how its contours should be cut.

There are many possible methods for enrichment of the surface of turned work, as with all woodwork. Transparent surface treatment protects the wood from dirt and accentuates its natural texture; rubbing with oil emphasises the grain and colour of the wood; staining and dyeing give it a new colour while still allowing the grain to show through. Coats of paint change the wood into a block of colour, obliterating its texture even to the extent of giving it the anonymity of a piece of plastic. This may be deliberate and legitimate, however, as it means that the grain and texture of the wood can no longer compete with its shape.

Books on the theory and practice of woodturning are no longer written only for professionals, but aim at making the craft accessible to amateurs.

This is the aim behind this book. The contents and presentation are intended to be accepted by professionals and to be understood by amateurs.

5

6

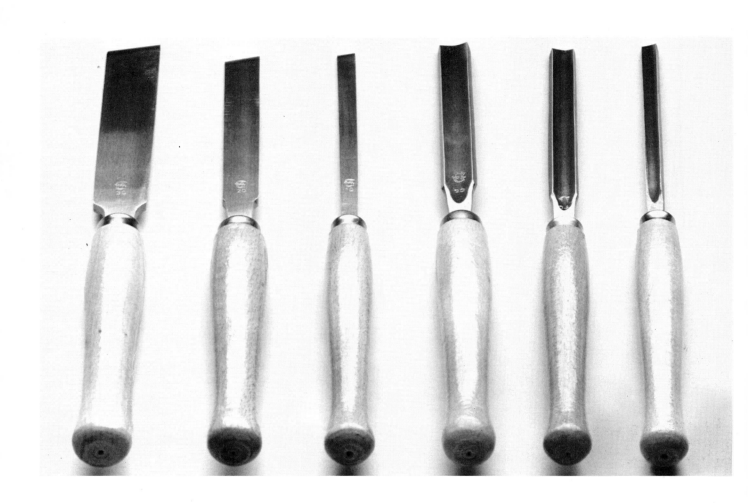

Materials and tools

Materials

The main material used for turning is wood, followed by ivory, plastics and metal. Wood has a special place in the hearts of both the professional and the amateur turner.

The technology of wood should be understood by all those who work with it. This is the only way to avoid mistakes and disappointments. Wood is a living material: it degrades, i.e. it dries and shrinks, and this must always be taken into account when working with it. Different species of native and foreign deciduous and coniferous wood differ in their hardness, density and colouring. These aspects must be considered when choosing a piece of wood to turn, as well as the function of the object to be made and its design.

Wood often has to be glued for technical, and also for aesthetic, reasons.

There are very large and heavy lathes available for professional turning and very light and reasonably-priced lathes for amateurs. The chucks used for mounting workpieces vary from simple screw and cup chucks to engineer's scroll chucks with up to six jaws.

The basic set of tools consists of only a few items. They should be well looked after, kept sharp and, most importantly, should be used skilfully. This, of course, requires practice — there is a good reason why professional turners undertake extensive training.

Measuring instruments, such as tape measures, vernier callipers and inside and outside callipers, are used to transfer drawings to the workpieces and to control measurements.

Special safety measures have been devised to prevent accidents and therefore should be carefully observed.

Sawn timber is the term given to pieces cut from the same trunk. Its use is limited to relatively small turnings.

Laminated wood consists of pieces of solid wood glued together. This removes the tension from the wood when very wide or thick pieces are required.

The advantages of wood are:
– variety of species
– beauty (grain and colour)
– elasticity
– toughness
– robustness
– ease of working

The disadvantages are that wood changes by swelling, shrinking, cracking and warping. These disadvantages may be reduced by appropriate cutting, gluing and careful workmanship, so that it is possible to produce flawless objects.

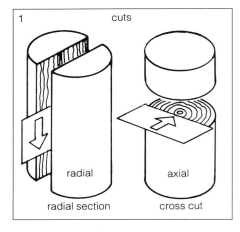

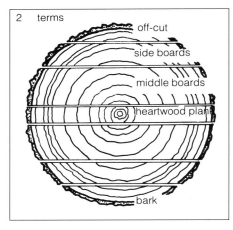

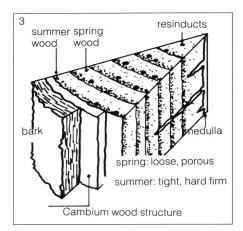

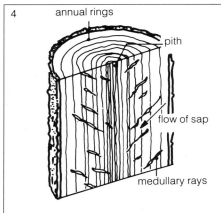

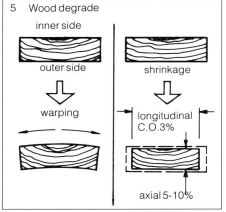

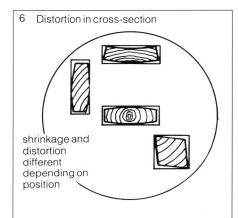

Pores are visible in the annual rings as small holes along which sap and water flow.

Medullary rays run from the centre of the trunk, or medulla. They radiate outwards, and are particularly easy to recognise in oak. Unlike pores, the rays form cross-connections which direct the sap from the outside to the middle of the trunk. Easily recognised in beech, oak and ash. Hardly recognisable in coniferous woods, lime, birch.

Softwood has no heartwood and is therefore light in tone.

Hardwood has both heart and sapwood and is thus both dark and light.

Mature wood is of varying degrees of hardness, but is entirely light in tone.

Sapwood has external annual rings. It is light, living, loose, young, and is of limited use for turning.

Heartwood is inside wood, and therefore dark, hard, firm, durable, old, good turning wood. The exceptions are the sapwood and the heartwood of conifers, both of which make good turning wood.

Mature wood trees show no visible difference between heart and sapwood, e.g. beech.

Wood degrade (the swelling and shrinkage) occurs when wood soaks up moisture (swelling) and releases it by evaporation (shrinkage). It expands and contracts even after its final finish.
When the annual rings lie in the wood it warps particularly badly. Standing annual rings are suitable for all joining and turning work. Accordingly, the

wood must be cut in such a way as to produce planks with as many upright rings as possible.
Longitudinal shrinkage (side grain) amounts to 0.3%. This is so mininal that it can be ignored, whereas radial shrinkage (end grain) may be up to 10%! This shrinkage must be taken into consideration when working.

Cracking: when wood dries too quickly it cracks and is unfit for turning. The inner side of the plank or board which faces the pith becomes convex on warping. The outer side of the board which faces the bark becomes concave.

Coniferous wood: light, not very firm, elastic, tough, easy to work.
In springtime large, light-coloured cells are produced. In the summer the cells produced are small and dark. Spring wood is therefore soft and loose, while summer wood is hard and firm.

Fig 10 shows the warping of a side plank. The wood always curves in the opposite direction to the annual rings. Fig 14 shows the spring growth of a piece of pine. Summer wood is darker and has smaller pores. Fig 8 shows the dark heart and light sapwood of a piece of oak.

Wood for turning must be free of knots. The shaded part of the piece of cherry-wood in Fig 11 must be removed.
Fig 12 shows excellent pieces of tuning wood: pine, palisander and mahogany.

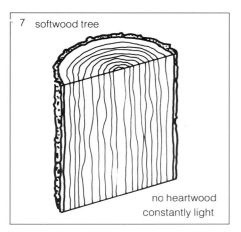

7 softwood tree

no heartwood
constantly light

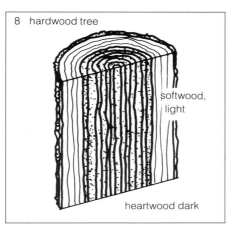

8 hardwood tree

softwood, light

heartwood dark

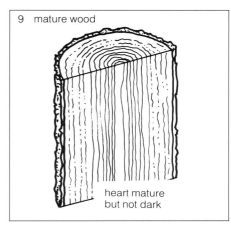

9 mature wood

heart mature but not dark

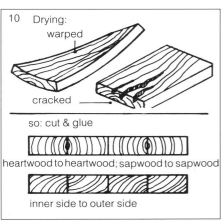

10 Drying:
warped

cracked

so: cut & glue

heartwood to heartwood; sapwood to sapwood

inner side to outer side

11

12

Deciduous wood: heavy, very firm, of varied texture, and more difficult to work than coniferous wood.

13

14

15

When fresh wood is seasoned the moisture content is reduced by approximately 10%. Seasoning occurs best in a slightly warmed shed. Sunshine and heat must be avoided, as they cause the wood to crack, which will make it useless. Six months' drying time is usually sufficient. As a general rule: 1 cm wood thickness requires one year's drying time when air-seasoned; less when dried artificially. It is advisable to keep a small supply of wood to hand.

Native and foreign coniferous and deciduous woods are listed below. Manufactured board, e.g. plywood, can also be used for turning. It has the advantage that it cannot warp, but a disadvantage is that it is difficult to turn because the glue between the crossed layers blunts tools quickly.

	Fir	Pine	Beech	Elm	Alder
workability	good, in spite of resin galls	good	good	difficult, due to brittle wood	easy, good
appearance	even lustre, light reddish structure	light sapwood yellowy-red heart, distinct annual rings	yellowish-white yellowish-red reddish-brown, few knots	light to dark brown grain similar to oak	light brown to reddish sapwood
qualities	high resin content many knots, soft wood	similar to fir, but less resin and fewer knots, soft wood	heavy, hard, very durable	tough, hard, elastic	light, soft, easily split, breaks easily
special features		beautiful shades on mellowing, not very suitable for staining	prone to woodworm, easy staining	beautiful shades on mellowing	very prone to woodworm, thus seldom used

	Poplar	Chestnut	Oak	Walnut	Cherry
workability	of limited use, as too soft	good, easier than oak	good; sharp tools important	good to very good	good
appearance	whitish to grey-white, reddish-yellow to greenish-brown; sap and heartwood	narrow sapwood, light brown heart	narrow sapwood (useless!); yellowish brown to yellowish red, light medullary rays	grey-white sapwood, brown heart, large pores	yellowish-white to reddish sapwood, reddish-yellow to reddish-brown heart, fine, small pores, heartwood
qualities	very soft and light, spongy	moderately hard, heavy	hard, very heavy, very durable and hardy	moderately heavy, hard	very heavy, hard, warps heavily
special features	good for painting	similar appearance to oak, but no medullary rays	expensive, heavy degrade (cracking); tanniferous – thus good for smoking	very fine and expensive, heavy shrinkage and cracking, polishes well	beautiful root grain; do not stain or oil, as this may cause marks

	Lime	Yew	Larch	Ash	Maple
workability	good, similar to alder	good	good to average	difficult	good
appearance	white sapwood, yellowish-white to reddish-white mature wood, inconspicuous grain	narrow, yellowish sapwood, wide, dark reddish-brown heart	sap and heartwood distinct, yellowy red colour	wide, yellowy-white sapwood, brown heart, green ash: greenish colour	yellow to white, fine structure, sapwood
qualities	light, soft, easy to work	heavy, hard, durable	heavy, very firm, little shrinkage	heavy, hard, very firm	moderately heavy, hard
special features	well suited for carving, painting and gilding	hardest coniferous wood, good for staining and polishing	relatively expensive, unsuitable for staining	lustrous, beautiful natural tones; do not stain!	demands little working, not prone to splitting, very suitable for fine work

	Apple	Birch	Tulipwood	Palisander	Teak
workability	good, similar to cherry and pear	good, easy, soft wood	good; contains toxic substances therefore unhealthy; rose scented!	difficult to work	good; sharp tools important
appearance	light sapwood, brownish heart	yellowish to reddish-white, flame-like veins, sapwood tree	rose-red to flesh pink, deep crimson	browny black, zebra-like grain	yellowish, grey-white sapwood, light brown heart
qualities	very hard and firm	soft, very tough, heavy degrade	very hard, brittle; small pores, easily split	similar to oak	hard; mineral deposits
special features	only suitable for small objects	expressive root grain, suitable for fine work	use for small, fine pieces, fades with time	very suitable for large works, plates and bowls	darkens on mellowing, weatherproof

	Pear	Ebony	Mahogany	Rosewood	Lignum Vitae
workability	good, similar to cherry	requires practice, due to danger of splitting	very good	good	good; gluing difficult
appearance	reddish brown; fine annual rings	almost black	yellow, brown, reddish to red; very varied grain	violet to dark brown, even black; very much varied, also in grain	light yellow sapwood, greenish, olive-brown heart
qualities	heavy, hard; hardly any degrade	very hard, brittle, splits easily	hard, heavy, firm, durable, needs little working	hard, heavy, somewhat brittle	heavy shrinkage and cracking, very hard
special features	beautiful root grain, polishes well	very valuable and expensive, polishes very well	mellows beautifully in warm shades; do not stain!	valuable and expensive; very beautiful colours	unpleasant smell; mellows to dark tone, suitable for 'heavy duty' goods, e.g. bowling balls

1 = larch

2 = ash

3 = oak

4 = walnut

5 = beech

6 = teak

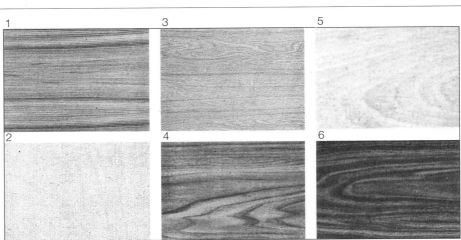

Large sections of wood are liable to crack during seasoning. To avoid this they are cut into smaller pieces, which removes the tension in the wood. Before the pieces are glued together again they must be planed so that the surfaces are even.

Long rods, e.g. for standard lamps with inside wiring, should be glued with the centre left hollow, which saves having to bore a hole afterwards. The two ends should be closed in so that they can be fixed between the lathe centres and bored open later.

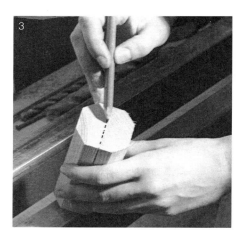

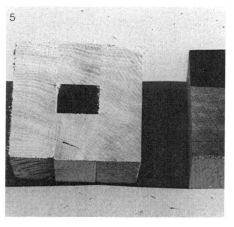

Both sides of the wood must be given a thin, even coat of glue and the parts pressed together with clamps, using cushions to prevent denting if necessary. If glue made of synthetic resin is used, the pieces will be firmly stuck together after about 30 minutes at room temperature (less time at a higher temperature).

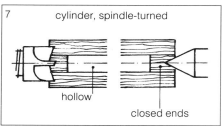

7 cylinder, spindle-turned

hollow

closed ends

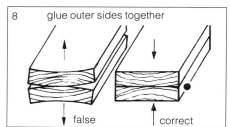

8 glue outer sides together

false | correct

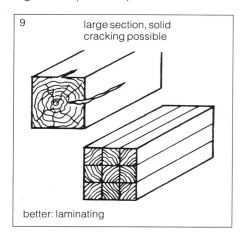

9 large section, solid cracking possible

better: laminating

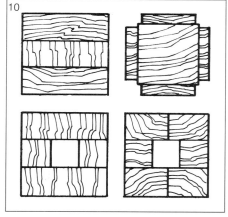

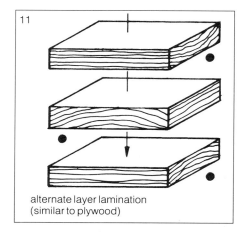

alternate layer lamination (similar to plywood)

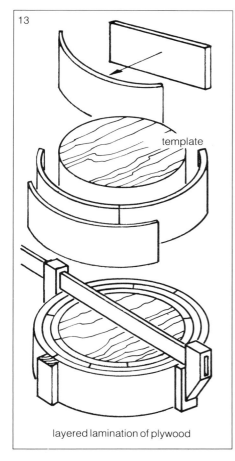

layered lamination of plywood

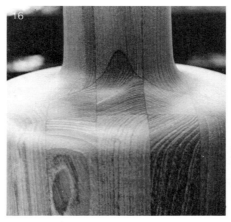

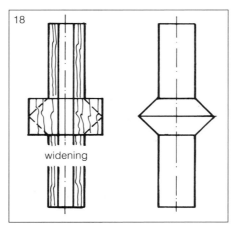

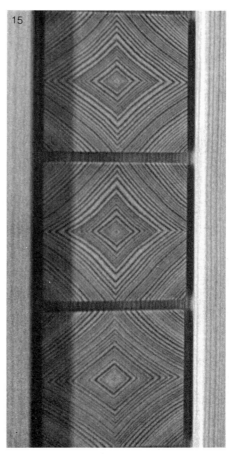

A frame can easily be made from thin pieces of plywood glued in layers round a wooden template. When the glue is dry the plywood keeps its shape and can be turned.
Interesting patterns and structures can be achieved by gluing pieces of wood together.

A wooden ball with a ring pattern can be turned from a square block to which small, veneer-like plates have been glued. Combining different types of wood, e.g. light and dark, increases the effect.

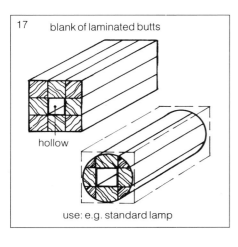

blank of laminated butts

hollow

use: e.g. standard lamp

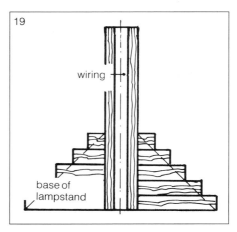

widening

wiring

base of lampstand

Apart from the actual turning tools, the lathe is the woodturner's most important item of equipment.

The lathe consists of: motor, headstock, bed, tailstock, and stand. It is driven by an electric motor next to the headstock. The motor has gears, which provides a range of speeds.

The gear unit consists of stepped pulleys with V-belts which can be interchanged according to the speed required.

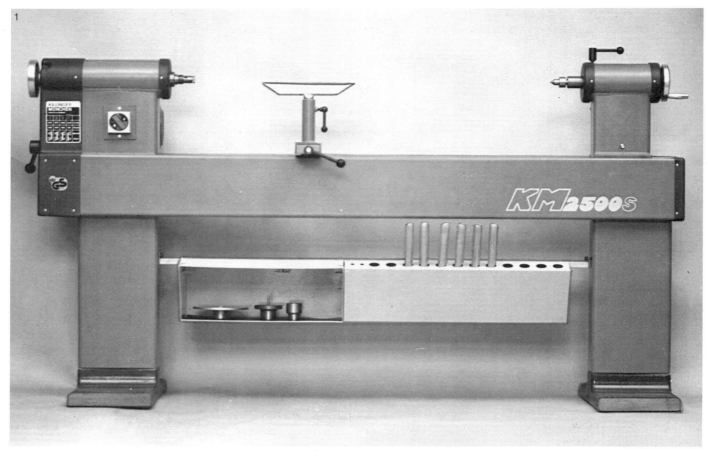

The lathe bed is made of cast iron, and the tailstock and the tool rest are mounted on it. The tailstock is the counterpart of the headstock and can be slid along the lathe bed.

The workpiece is usually mounted firmly between the headstock and tailstock centres (spindle-turning).

In the tailstock there is a spindle for attaching a lathe centre or a boring attachment. The spindle is moved in and out by a handwheel. It can be fixed in a particular position with a locking lever.

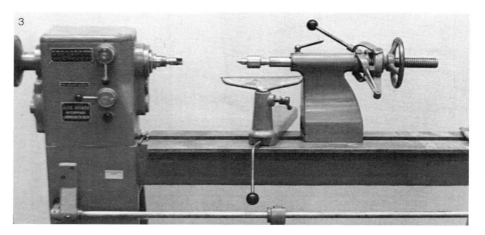

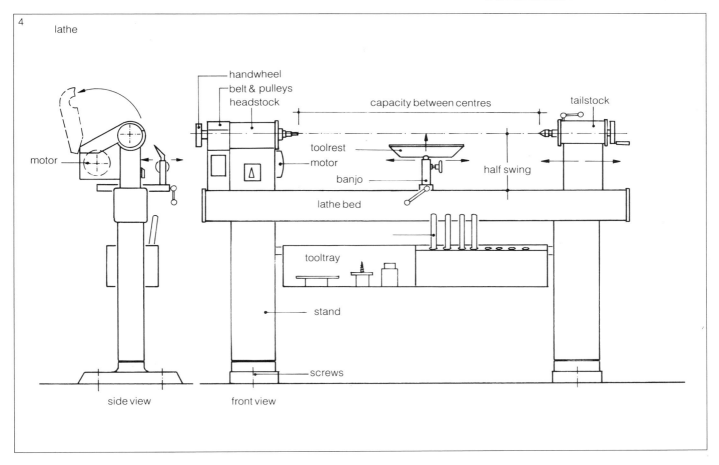

4   lathe

handwheel
belt & pulleys
headstock
capacity between centres
tailstock
motor
toolrest
motor
banjo
half swing
lathe bed
tooltray
stand
screws

side view   front view

The tool rest serves to guide the turning tool, which is held up against it. The height of the tool rest is adjustable; it is held in a stand, usually called a banjo. It can also be positioned at right angles to the bed for face-plate turning.

The stand is the base of the lathe and supports both headstock and bed. It is made of cast iron and can be bolted to the floor. In large machines the stand, headstock and bed are cast together as one unit.

In order to turn large discs or plates, lathes with a recessed bed are necessary (see Fig 6). Headstocks with a spindle thread on both sides allow outboard turning of discs or the attachment of a grinding or polishing wheel.

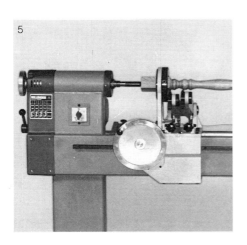

5

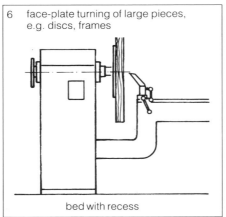

6   face-plate turning of large pieces, e.g. discs, frames

bed with recess

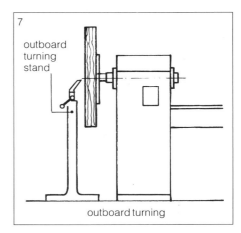

7

outboard turning stand

outboard turning

The following information is intended to help those buying a lathe for small-scale commercial production or for amateur woodturning work.

Important points to consider are: capacity between centres, distance of the centres above the bed (swing), motor capacity, speed control (belt or electronic), free-standing or bench-top model, working life, quality of workmanship, intended purpose, additional equipment available, price, and guarantee.

The **capacity between centres** is the maximum possible distance between the headstock and tailstock centres. It should be about 1000 mm in order to turn such things as spindles for stairways.

The **distance of the centres above the bed** (swing) is the maximum distance between the upper edge of the bed and the centre axis. In general a radius of 200 mm is adequate. This enables a bowl with a diameter of 350 to 400 mm to be turned.

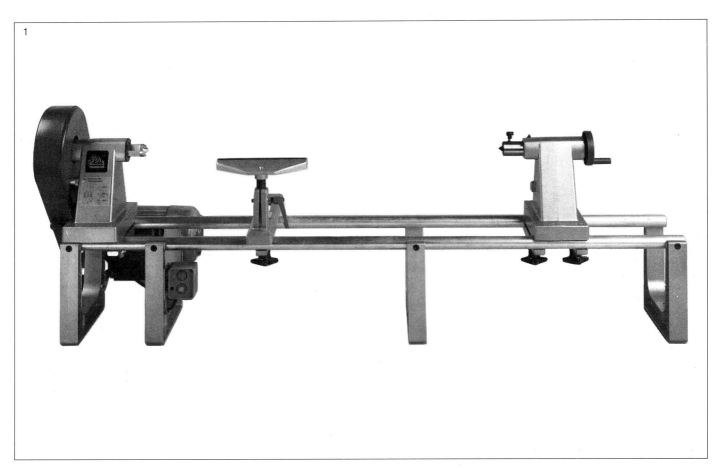

1

The **motor capacity** varies from model to model, but is usually between 500 and 1000 watts. It is often possible to choose between direct (380 v) and alternating (220 v) current.

Stand The lighter type of lathe may be used with or without a stand. In many cases a stable support is sufficient.

Sturdiness varies. It is advisable to compare several models. Make sure that the lathe bed is stable! Ask for the machine to be demonstrated and look for the British Standards Institution 'kite mark'.

Intended purpose Consider what you intend to use the lathe for. Different models and capacities are needed for hobby or commercial work, and you may even require copy-

ing equipment. A simple, small machine is suitable for amateur use.

Additional equipment A wide assortment of additional equipment is available. However, this usually has to be specially ordered. Equipment produced by one firm does not always fit on another firm's lathe.

The **working life** of a lathe depends very much on the way it is used and looked after.

The workpieces should always be well centred, i.e. not offcentre, to avoid vibration or jolting. In the long run this would have a negative effect on the bearings in the headstock. From time to time all the moving parts must be greased lightly so that the tailstock or the tool rest, for example, can slide along the bed easily. The lathe must be kept as free as possible of wood dust and shavings.

Guarantee Always make sure that the lathe has a guarantee.

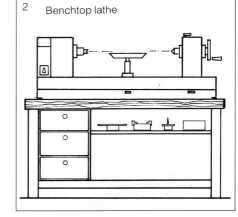

2 Benchtop lathe

The lathe bed in Fig 1 consists of two tubular steel bars. The tailstock spindle is hollow, allowing easier boring of long axial holes, e.g. for the wiring in a standard lamp stand. The lathe is light and convenient, and weighs about 32 kg.

Fig 3 shows a smaller type of lathe with three speeds. The motor is mounted behind the headstock and may be swung back or forward to change the belt from one pulley to another for a different speed.

The position of the belt for the various speeds is shown on a small metal plate. The smaller the diameter of the workpiece, the higher the speed.

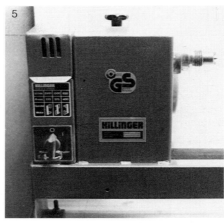

The are a number of chucks in use for holding wooden workpieces. They are usually made of steel and available from the same firms as the lathe. Homemade, wooden chucks make extensive, specialised work possible.

Driving centres, screw, cup and engineer's chucks and faceplates should be all that are needed for most work. A driving centre with three or four prongs, or spurs, is used in spindle-turning (Figs 1 and 7). It is screwed into the headstock spindle, and the prongs grip into the end grain of the workpiece.

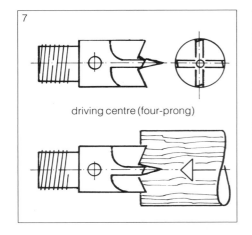

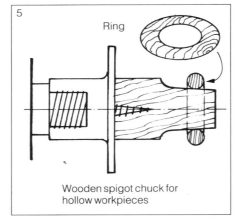

Fig 5: Wooden spigot chuck for hollow workpieces — Ring

The tail centre is the counterpart of the driving centre and is mounted in the tailstock. Live centres are also available – these are tail centres with a ball-bearing that spin as the wood turns.

The screw chuck (Figs 2 and 9) is a faceplate with a wood screw. Small to medium-sized workpieces, e.g.

bowls, can be screwed to it.

Before using a cup chuck (Figs 4 and 8) the end of the workpiece must be tapered so that it can be pressed firmly against the chuck's inner walls. The workpiece must be wedged into position with a hammer.

The inside of the chuck is slightly grooved, giving a better grip on the workpiece.

The faceplate (Figs 3 and 13) is a metal disc with slits or radial rows of screw-holes. Large workpieces, e.g. plates or bowls, can be screwed firmly and securely to a faceplate. The disc can also also have abrasive paper glued to it so that it can be used for sanding.

Fig 7: driving centre (four-prong)

Fig 8: Cup-chuck — steel — wood

Fig 9: screw chuck

A steady is used to support long, slender, spindle-turned workpieces. This helps to reduce the whipping motion which could otherwise be caused by the long piece of wood bowing between the two centres. The steady can be adjusted according to the size of the workpiece.

10

11

Steadies as simple supports can also be homemade from a piece of wood. Long rods, e.g. for standard lamps with inside wiring, should be laminated and the centre left hollow to save having to bore a hole afterwards. Only the two ends should be closed in, so that they can be mounted

between the lathe centres; they can be bored open later.
The three- or `four-jawed engineer's scroll chuck (Figs 10–12 and 15) is used for mounting workpieces that are to be either spindle or faceplate turned. The workpiece is automatically centred when the jaws are

set. A chuck key is used to tighten the jaws. Appropriately-shaped jaws must be used for a flush sit, gripping either from the inside or outside.

Fig 3: A faceplate with screw holes, homemade from a synthetic plate, is mounted on a screw chuck.

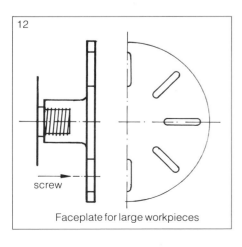

12

screw

Faceplate for large workpieces

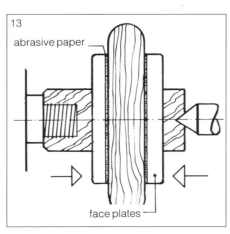

13

abrasive paper

face plates

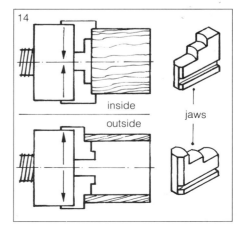

14

inside

outside

jaws

There is a great variety of woodturning tools. For a basic set, however, five different items are sufficient:
– roughing gouge
– hollowing gouge
– skew chisel
– flat chisel
– parting tool

The **gouge** is the most frequently used turning tool. It is used to shape blanks (which are usually sawn square) down to cylinders. It is used in both spindle and faceplate turning. The cutting edge is rounded and bevelled at 30°.

The **skew chisel** is used for V-cuts, beads and conical shapes. It is used for smoothing and the turner can cut or scrape with it. Skews are available with a bevel on one or both sides. The cutting edge has an angle of 70°.

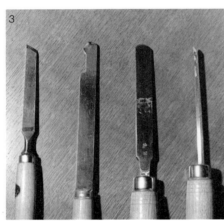

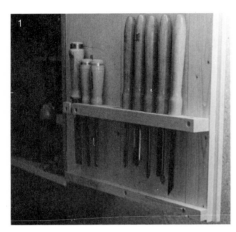

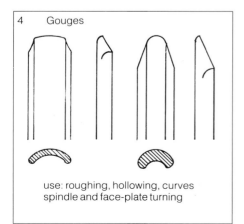

The **spindle gouge** is a detail gouge usually used in faceplate turning. It is used for scraping and, in spindle-turning, for cutting hollows. In general the spindle gouge is used for pre-liminary turning. Like the roughing gouge, it has a rounded cutting edge which is bevelled at 40°.

A **flat chisel** can be used for on-the-lathe finishing. It has a bevel ground on one side at an angle of 25°.

The **parting tool** is used for cutting or scraping squared shoulders and grooves. Its cross-section measures between 4 mm and 6 mm, the sectional view is flat and rectangular.

To prevent friction between the tool and the workpiece, the side is trapezium-shaped in cross-section. These tools can be bought either individually or in sets.

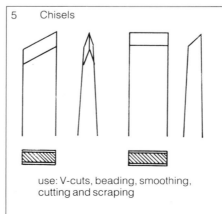

4 Gouges

use: roughing, hollowing, curves spindle and face-plate turning

5 Chisels

use: V-cuts, beading, smoothing, cutting and scraping

6 Flat chisels

use: planing, spindle-turning

Specialised turning tools. Scrapers are used to make hollows, found in bowls and jars. An appropriately-shaped scraper will reach parts which another cannot. Simple, relatively standardised shapes are available from specialised dealers. The professional turner usually has them specially made by a toolmaker or a smith.

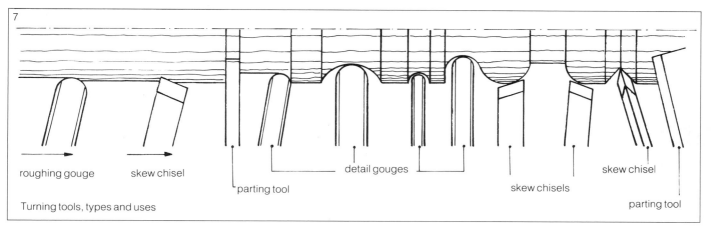

roughing gouge   skew chisel

detail gouges

skew chisel

parting tool

skew chisels

parting tool

Turning tools, types and uses

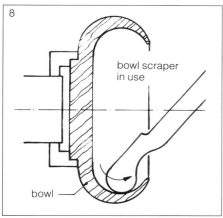

8

bowl scraper in use

bowl

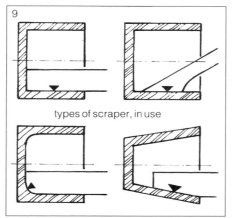

9

types of scraper, in use

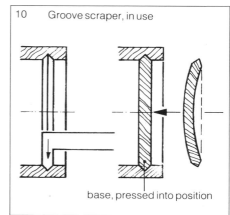

10   Groove scraper, in use

base, pressed into position

These specialised tools are difficult to handle and are not recommended for use by the amateur turner.
There are also bent scrapers, used for cutting grooves on inside walls (Fig 10); these tools, too, are recommended only for use by professionals.

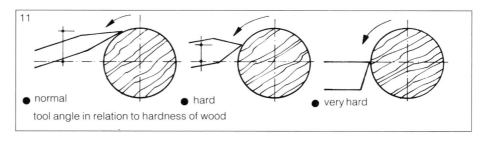

11

● normal   ● hard   ● very hard

tool angle in relation to hardness of wood

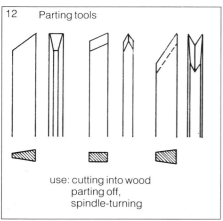

12   Parting tools

use: cutting into wood
parting off,
spindle-turning

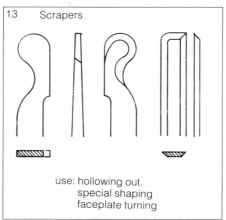

13   Scrapers

use: hollowing out.
special shaping
faceplate turning

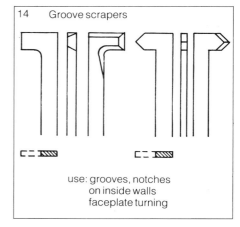

14   Groove scrapers

use: grooves, notches
on inside walls
faceplate turning

Grinding the turning tools. Good results can only be obtained if well-sharpened turning tools are used. If the angles of the cutting edges are incorrect, or if they are blunt, tools must be ground and then honed.

A two-wheel bench dry-grinder, with a coarse and a fine grinding wheel, is adequate for this. It should be firmly screwed down on a workbench or strong table. It is important to have a wheel guard to protect against flying sparks, and tool rests which are large enough for the tool being worked on. Safety goggles should always be worn.

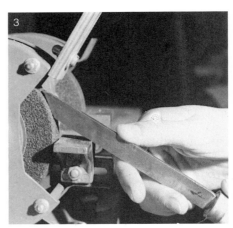

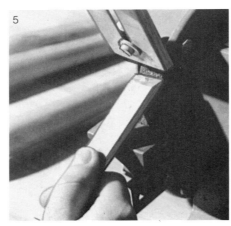
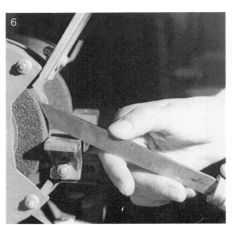

Gouges must be turned to and fro against the grinding wheel until the bevel (cutting edge) is sharp (approx. 30°). Then the entire heel of the bevel should fit against the wheel, and its edges merge evenly into the bevel.

Chisels with long cutting edges are first held with the heel of the bevel up against the grindstone, and moved from side to side. When one bevel is straight, the chisel is turned over to sharpen the other bevel (see Fig 12).

Parting tools have a bevel of 25°. In this case too, first the heel is held against the grindstone, then the handle is lifted slightly until the correct angle is obtained.

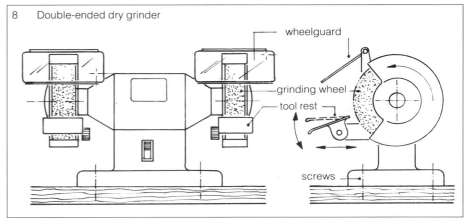

8   Double-ended dry grinder

wheelguard

grinding wheel

tool rest

screws

Large abrasive discs on a lathe allow face or angular grinding of wooden edges or surfaces. They cannot be used for sharpening tools, however.

9

10   mechanical wheel dresser

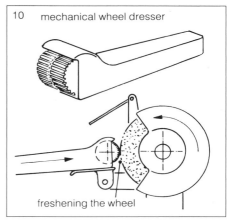

freshening the wheel

11

12

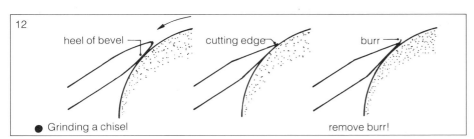

heel of bevel   cutting edge   burr

● Grinding a chisel   remove burr!

Grinding wheels come in a number of grades, similar to sandpaper. Bond and structure are also important. Those wheels marked with a **V**, and which contain ceramic bonding, are preferable. The grain should be medium coarse, the bond hard to very hard and the structure open.

The blade of a tool should not turn blue while being sharpened, as this changes and damages the structure of the metal so that the blade blunts more quickly afterwards. Tools may be cooled down in water after being sharpened.

As grinding wheels wear down, they should be freshened and trued from time to time. This is best done with a mechanical dresser, which is held up against the wheel to roughen it.

The grain of grinding wheels:

very coarse	8 – 12
coarse	14 – 24
medium coarse	30 – 60
fine	70 – 120
very fine	150 – 240
extra fine	280 – 600

Structure:

slightly open	1 – 4
open	5 – 8
very open	9 – 12
porous	13 – 16
very porous	17 – 20

Bond:

very weak	E, F, G, H
weak	I, J, K, L
medium strong	M, N, 0
strong	P, Q, R
very strong	S, T, U, V

Honing the turning tools: After they have been ground the tools are honed on a slipstone. Distinctions are made between oil, Arkansas and Mississippi stones (named after their places of origin). These must be handled with care, as they can break easily.

The slipstones are kept either on a special wooden support, or in a glass of water or paraffin so that they stay nicely moist. The particular features of various stones are different hardness and grain. Arkansas stones are the best and are used most often.

Slipstones are shaped according to the tool they are intended for, i.e. they are either flat, rectangular or rounded and fit against the blade of the tool.

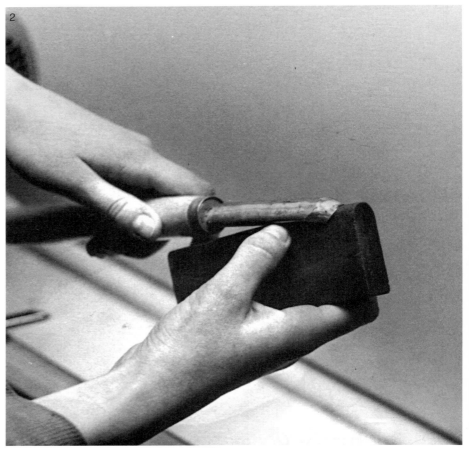

The gouge is pressed against the stone and rubbed in a circular motion. The stone must occasionally be moistened with paraffin. The gouge must be moved as far to the right as it is to the left, so that the entire cutting edge is sharpened. The inside of the gouge is pulled along the curved

edge of the slipstone. This process is repeated until the burr has disappeared.

Once the tools have been honed they must be cleaned very carefully with wood shavings, which remove the paraffin and grinding dust.

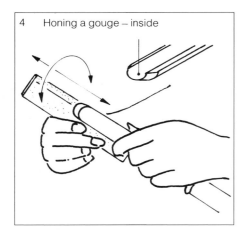

4 Honing a gouge – inside

5 Honing a skew chisel

6 Honing a gouge – outside

When a skew chisel is honed it is pressed flat against the stone and rubbed against it in a circular motion. A fine burr appears on the cutting edge, caused by the grinding. Then the other bevel must be honed. This process is repeated until the cutting edge is flawless and has no burr. The entire heel of the bevel must lie flat on the slipstone.

The parting tool is also honed by being rubbed in a circular motion. As the cross-section of the blade is so small, great care must be taken not to dent or score the stone.

The use of measuring equipment is essential in woodturning. Instruments are used to measure and check the length, width, thickness of the sides, diameter, contours and surface of a piece of wood.

A yardstick is important for measuring length and for setting dividers at a particular measurement. A ruler will often be adequate.
Tape measures are small, practical and convenient. They are very useful for measuring the circumference of a cylinder.

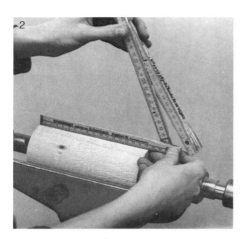

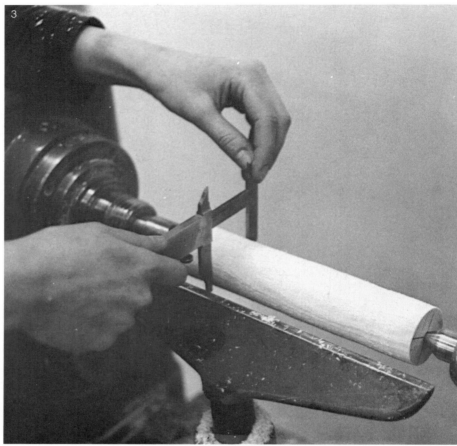

Dividers are used for copying the measurements of a drawing onto the workpiece in a 1 : 1 scale, as well as for tracing or marking. They also serve to plot arcs on blanks that are to be used for bowls or plates.

Dividers with curved legs and an adjustment screw are suitable for copying measurements while the workpiece is moving. The rotation transfers the line to the workpiece as required.

Callipers are used for inside and outside measurements, as well as for measuring the thickness of sides. They are only used when the lathe is not in motion.

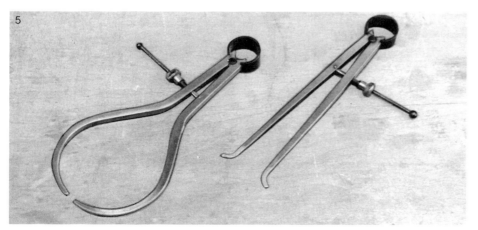

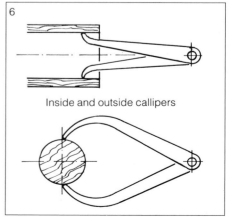

Inside and outside callipers

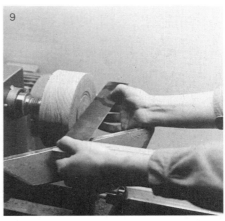

Vernier callipers can be used universally and are very precise. Diameters, lengths, inside measurements and depths can be checked to within 1/10 mm. They must be handled carefully and should be kept lightly greased so that the vernier can be moved easily.

Joiners' try-squares, made of wood or metal, are used to check angles and surfaces. Some of these have millimetre divisions.

Templates are usually only used for copying. They are held up against the contours of the workpiece. The templates can be homemade from cardboard, wood or plastic.

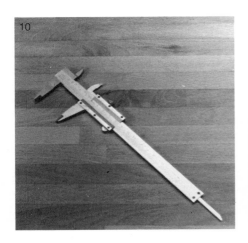

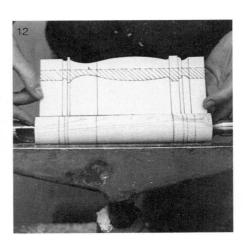

Additional tools are needed if you are going to prepare wood for turning, unless you can buy appropriately sawn, planed or dressed wood.
The varied assortment of machines and tools available leaves practically no desire unfulfilled.

Band and circular saws are generally all the amateur needs. It is important that the saws have adjustable tables and fences so that blanks can be cut at angles before turning.
If wood is to be laminated, the pieces must first be quite smooth and even. A planing and a thicknessing machine are required for this.

Combined machines save buying a whole range. One machine can perform several functions, e.g. both planing and thicknessing or both sawing and moulding. The machines must be specially adjusted for each function, however.

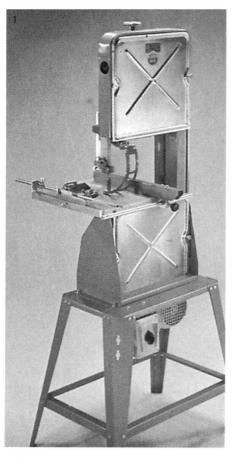

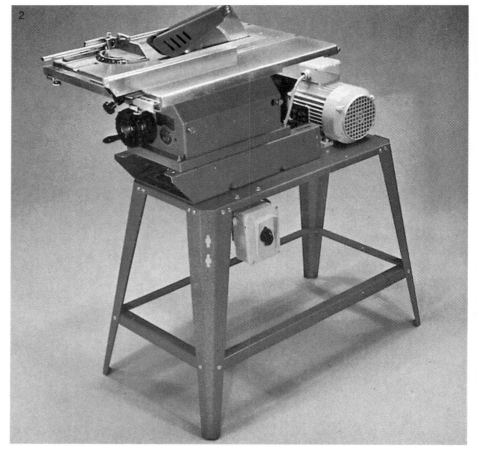

With a bandsaw, very thick boards can be cut either straight or curved with no great physical effort. The width of cut is about 1.2 mm and the height about 150 mm.
Objects with a large diameter, e.g. plates and bowls, can be cut roughly to shape with a bandsaw.

Depending on the thickness of the wood, the roller bearing should be set just above the wood's surface to prevent it from bending too much when the wood is pushed along.

The circular saw is used to cut solid timber to size. Saw blades made of chrome vanadium are adequate. Depending on the diameter, they have 8, 12 or 16 teeth, which are not tipped with carbide metal. For precision work carbide metal-tipped blades should be used. These also cut tropical woods cleanly.

A workbench with vices, a well and a drawer is ideal for preparing and finishing turned work. It is also very useful for other forms of woodwork. The tools required are: tenon saw, handsaw, hammer, awl, screwdriver, plane and C-clamps. A grinder is recommended for sharpening the turning tools.

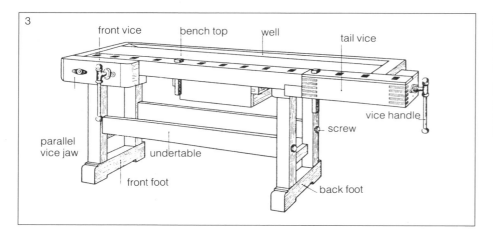

front vice bench top well tail vice
vice handle
parallel vice jaw
undertable
screw
front foot
back foot

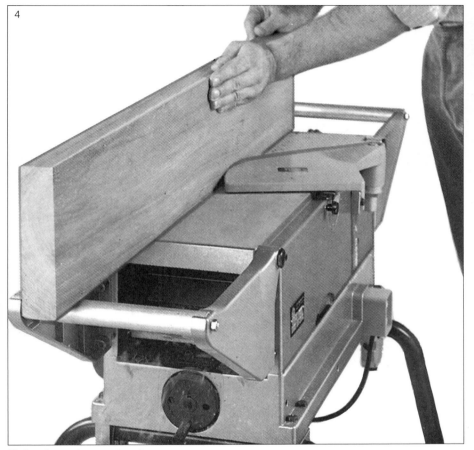

Rules for using a circular saw:
1. Always use a riving knife.
2. The blade should not show further than about 2 mm through the cut wood.
3. Avoid side friction; do not tilt the wood.
4. Use a push stick.
5. Do not remove the guard from the saw blade.

A planing machine levels curved, uneven areas on boards or squared wood. The cutter block planes off the excess wood. Planing machines have a fence at the edge and adjustable guards for the cutter blocks (see Figs 4, 5, 6). If possible, wood should only be pushed in the direction of the grain so that the surface does not split.

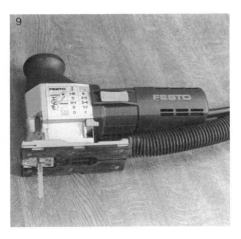

1. Ensure there is adequate lighting. The lathe should stand by a window and have fluorescent lighting installed above it.
2. Do not leave unnecessary objects in the working area! Keep your workplace tidy.
3. Install electric connections and switches according to the instructions. Connect the earth wire correctly. Do not trap wires.

Safety measures are taken to help prevent accidents. Working at a lathe with rotating workpieces and sharp tools demands care and caution. If a few basic rules and safety precautions are observed, woodturning is a relatively safe occupation.

4. Only open the access door to change pulleys when the lathe is switched off.
5. Roll up sleeves! Chains, rings, watches, etc. should always be taken off before starting work.
6. Long hair should be kept back in a cap or hairnet.

7. Set the tool rest at the correct height and distance from the workpiece.
8. Hold the turning tools at the correct angle.
9. Choose the correct speed for the size and hardness of the wood.

10. Saw large pieces of wood into rounds or octagons before turning.
11. Measure and check the workpiece only when the lathe is not moving.

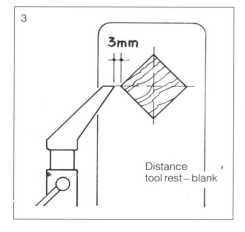

3mm

Distance
tool rest – blank

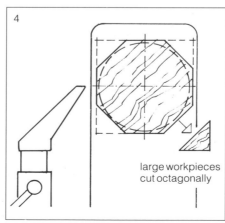

large workpieces
cut octagonally

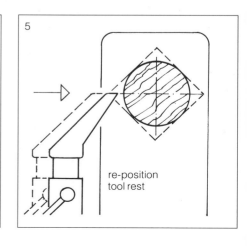

re-position
tool rest

Turning must always be done at the correct speed. The workpiece must be securely mounted. Large blanks mounted on faceplates must be secured with sufficiently long screws. When engineer's chucks are used, care must be taken to ensure that the jaws fit flush to the workpiece.

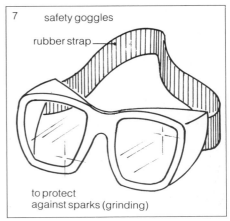

7 safety goggles

rubber strap

to protect
against sparks (grinding)

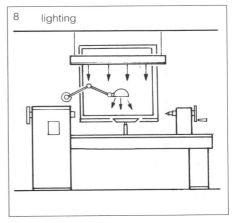

8 lighting

Extremely long and slender work-pieces which are spindle-turned have a tendency to sag between centres and then whip away. The use of a steady to support the middle of the work prevents such accidents.

When large workpieces are faceplate turned, and during cup chuck turning, the turner should stand to the right of the workpiece, so that it cannot fly out at him. **NB** The workpiece always rotates *towards* the tool and the turner.

Laminated workpieces should be glued very carefully on both sides, as the centrifugal force of the lathe could otherwise burst them apart. Low speeds of about 800 rpm should always be chosen for this type of work.

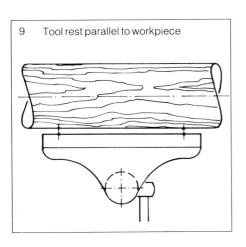

9 Tool rest parallel to workpiece

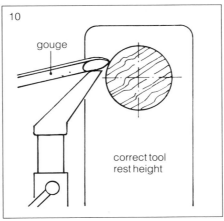

10 gouge

correct tool
rest height

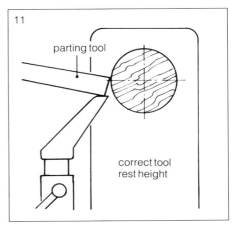

11 parting tool

correct tool
rest height

Technique

Spindle-turning

This is the most commonly-used method of turning.

The grain of the wood runs parallel to the centre of rotation.
The workpiece is mounted at both ends.

Preparation includes choosing the type of wood, cutting it to size and laminating large or specially-shaped pieces.

A cylinder is turned by simple scraping or by somewhat more difficult cutting, using a roughing gouge and a skew chisel.

Hollows of various sizes are cut with a gouge.

V-cuts and chamfers are cut with a skew chisel.

Shoulders are squared with a parting tool, 'male' V-cuts with a skew chisel or a gouge.

To turn beads, four markings must first be cut. The beads are then shaped with a detail gouge.

Ogee is the term used to describe a contour that comprises a long, S-shaped curve which gradually changes from a hollow to a bead. These shapes are very interesting, as they can be made individually by the turner according to his own ideas and ability.

Spindle-turning is the most popular form of turning. Basic shapes such as cylinders, hollows, V-cuts, chamfers, squared shoulders, beads and ogees can all be experimented with to gain basic experience.

Simple everyday objects, e.g. candlesticks or skipping-rope handles, can be made as soon as the turner is familiar with both tools and wood, after constant practice. Gradually, other objects which require more experience can be produced.

Part of the preparation process for spindle-turning involves the cutting of blanks. When the required measurements are known and the type of wood has been chosen, the blank is cut roughly to shape with a circular saw or a bandsaw.
The wood must be free from knotholes, dry, not warped and not contain any cracks. It is usually enough to saw the blank to a rectangle before spindle-turning. If the diameter is greater than 10 cm, the edges should be sawn off with a bandsaw (Fig 9). If the blank is too long for the bandsaw, a circular saw with an adjustable blade should be used.

Removal of the edges prevents the roughing gouge from repeatedly hitting the wood.

Fig 2 shows a rectangular pinewood blank alongside two roughed cylinders, tapered at one end.
The tapered end will later be driven into a cup chuck (Fig 3).

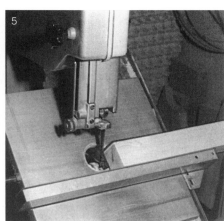

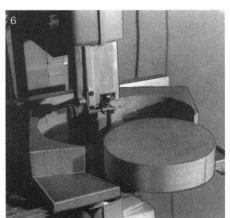

Figs 4-6 show preparation of wood with a bandsaw. By sloping the bandsaw table, the sides of the blank can be cut at an angle. Large pieces of wood can be cut to a disc.

Fig 8 shows a piece of pine which has a split in the centre. Only the piece to the right and left of the split can be used for turning.

Once the wood has been chosen and cut to a rectangle it should be turned down to a cylinder. To do this the centre of both cross-cut ends must be established so that the piece can be mounted between the driving and tail centres.

The central point can be found by drawing diagonals (Fig 4). When hardwood is used, the point is marked with a centre punch so that the driving and tail centres have a better grip. The workpiece is then mounted, and the tailstock with the tail centre is pushed towards it.

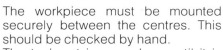

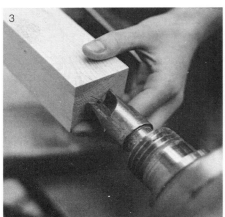

The workpiece must be mounted securely between the centres. This should be checked by hand.
The tool rest is moved up until it is about 3 mm away from the blank. It is important to ensure that the edges of the blank cannot hit against the tool rest, which must be parallel to it.

Work begins using a roughing gouge. Starting with light roughing at around 1200 rpm, the gouge is moved continuously from left to right along the workpiece and back again, without using a great deal of pressure.

The cylindrical shape is smoothed using a skew chisel. This is held at an angle of 25°-30° to the workpiece and is moved from left to right and back again. The surface quality should be examined with the lathe switched off. It must be re-worked if necessary.

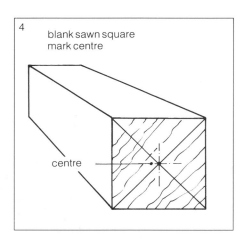

4
blank sawn square
mark centre

centre

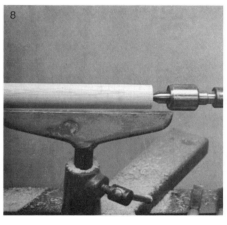

There is a distinction betwen cutting and planing. In general, cutting is done with a gouge and planing with a skew chisel.

Cutting is simple and requires relatively little practice. Planing is more difficult, but quicker and cleaner. It is possible to tell from the shavings whether the wood has been cut or planed. Cut shavings are short and flaky, while planed shavings are long and fine. When wood is cut the shavings spring off; when it is planed they peel away in spirals.

Figs 5 and 9 show the difference: shawings on the left are cut, and those on the right are planed. With both methods it is essential to use good, well-sharpened tools.

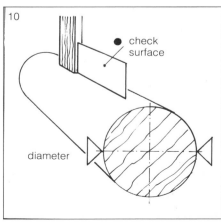

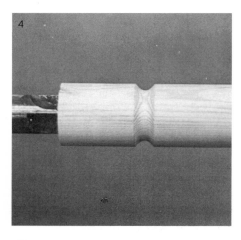

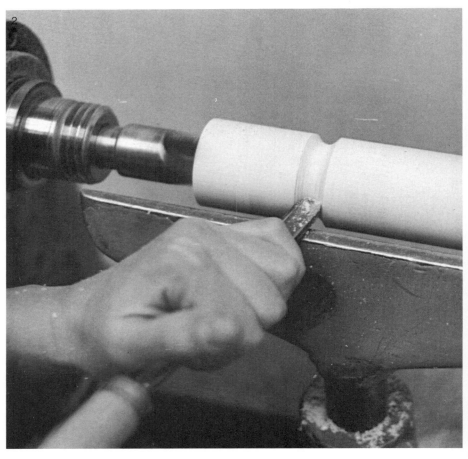

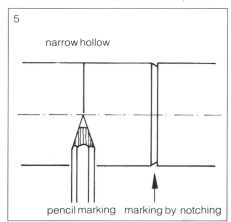

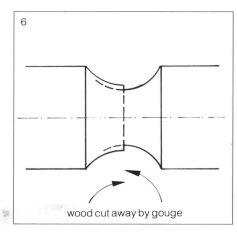

The turning of a narrow hollow is shown here. When the blank has been turned to a cylinder and smoothed, markings about 2 cm apart are made on it (Figs 1 and 5).

The hollow is cut between the markings with a gouge (Fig 3). During cutting the gouge is moved towards the markings to the left and right using gentle pressure (Fig 6).

Once the rough shape has been established, the gouge is pushed alternately from each line towards the centre of the hollow and turned until it fits evenly into it (Fig 2). A hollow is worked from the outside to the centre, but no further.

narrow hollow

pencil marking   marking by notching

wood cut away by gouge

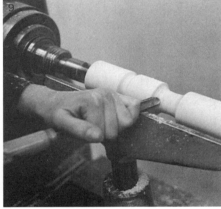

A wide hollow or spool is made by working two narrow hollows next to each other so that a ridge is formed where they meet.

The ridge is cut away with a gouge (Figs 10 and 11). The rough shape is completed by repeatedly moving the gouge from the outsides to the centre. It must be sanded afterwards.

Figs 7, 8, 9 and 12 show the contrast between narrow and wide hollows. Figs 10 and 11 show the motion of the gouge.

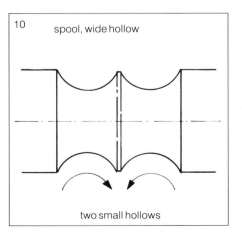

spool, wide hollow

two small hollows

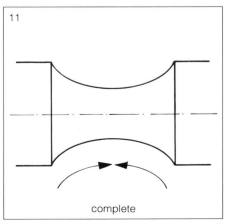

complete

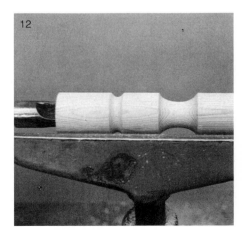

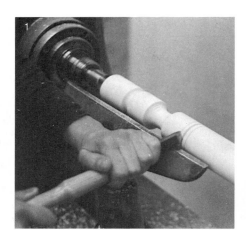

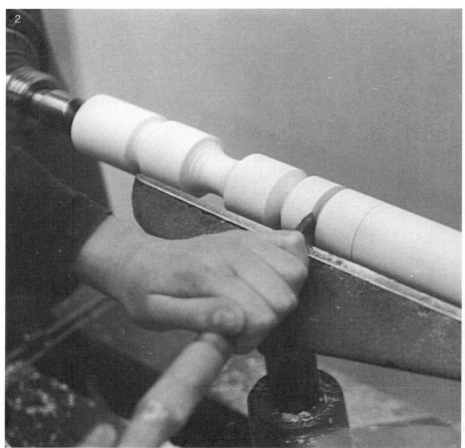

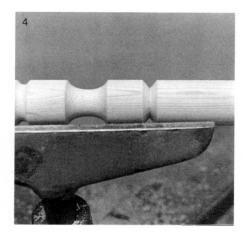

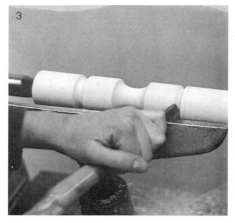

A skew chisel is used to make 'female' V-cuts. After the width of the cut has been marked, a fine indentation is cut in the centre. Wood is removed from both sides, working towards the central notch until the markings are reached.

V-cuts are worked from the centre outwards, in the opposite direction to that used when working hollows.
Both sides of the V must be straight and meet exactly in the centre.

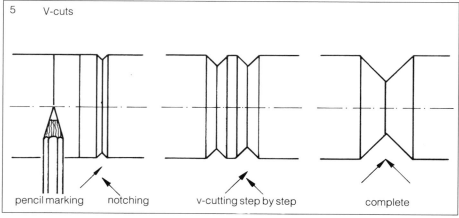

5   V-cuts

pencil marking   notching   v-cutting step by step   complete

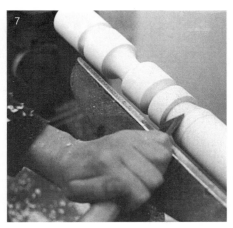

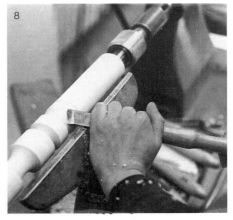

Cutting chamfers is a similar process to making hollows. As usual, the required width is marked beforehand. One side is vertical, however, and the other diagonal.

After the vertical cut has been made, the diagonal is cut little by little with a skew chisel until the marking is reached and the angle is correct.

Next, the shoulder must be smoothed. For this the skew is held so that only its tip removes wood and the heel of the bevel stays on the tool rest.

Fig 4 shows the comparison between a V-cut and hollows.
Fig 9 shows the comparison between a V-cut and a chamfer.

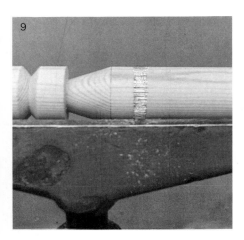

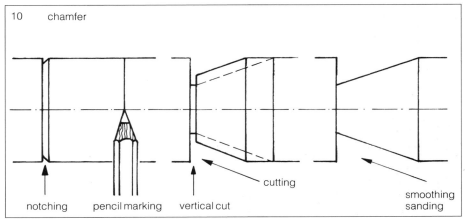

10   chamfer

notching   pencil marking   vertical cut   cutting   smoothing sanding

A parting tool is used for squaring shoulders. It is held against the wood and carefully pushed into it.

The sides of the recess can be cut very cleanly with a parting tool. Wood on cross-cut surfaces can also be parted off well with it.

Fig 4 shows the rough shape of a serviette ring.

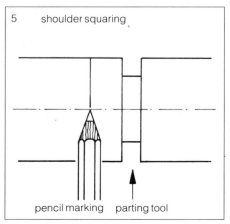

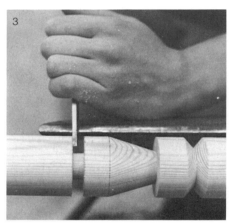

pencil marking   parting tool

cutting parallel, smoothing

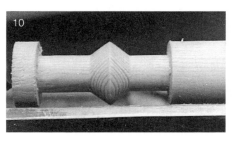

Turning 'male' V-cuts requires a fair degree of skill. The two outer markings must first be slightly notched with a skew, then the wood is cut away with a gouge on the left and right until the tip of the V is reached. The V is then turned using a skew chisel.

It is very important that the two pins cut away at the left and right of the V are level and that the tip of the V does not shift position.

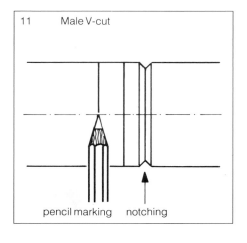

11 Male V-cut

pencil marking   notching

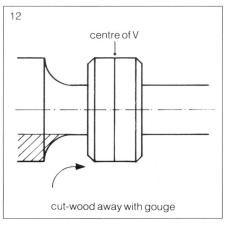

12

centre of V

cut-wood away with gouge

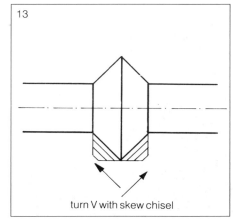

13

turn V with skew chisel

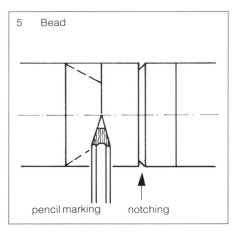

Four markings need to be made before turning a bead. A diagonal is cut from each of the two outer markings and the piece in the centre is rounded.

To accentuate the bead, the diagonals must be cut sufficiently wide and deep to give the tool enough room for movement.

Fig 2 shows the two completed diagonals to the left and right of the bead. The edges are carefully rounded off with a detail gouge. Particular care must be taken to ensure that the blade does not slip and damage the diagonals.

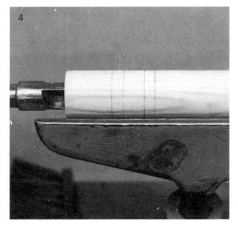

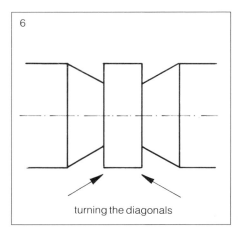

5 Bead

pencil marking   notching

6

turning the diagonals

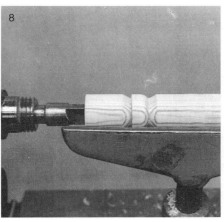

The bead is formed by repeatedly moving the gouge from the centre towards the diagonals until the correct roundness is achieved. The bead is then smoothed with a skew chisel.
Fig 13 shows a completed bead. The interrupted course of the wood grain gives an interesting effect.

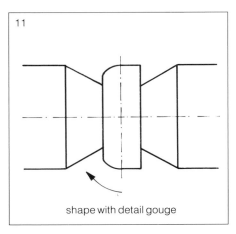

shape with detail gouge

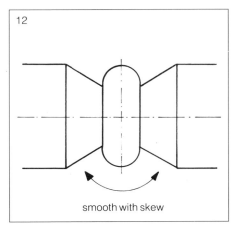

smooth with skew

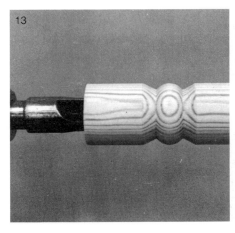

An ogee consists of two basic shapes which merge together: a bead and a hollow. Depending on how marked a contour is required, either a gouge or a skew chisel is used. If the curve is long and drawn out, a skew can be used. If it is compact and well rounded, a gouge is better.

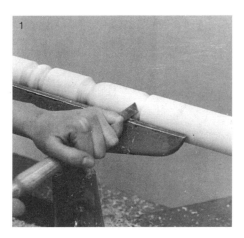

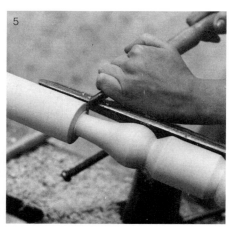

In Figs 1-5 the ogee is worked with a skew chisel. The way in which the bead merges into the hollow, the extent of its roundness and the contour of the curve as a whole are a matter of feeling.

Designing ogee forms is a particularly attractive task, as it allows so much scope for the turner's own sense of shape.

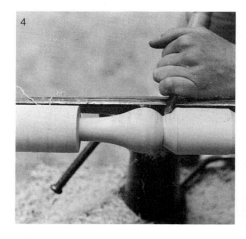

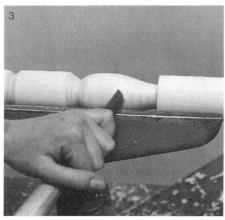

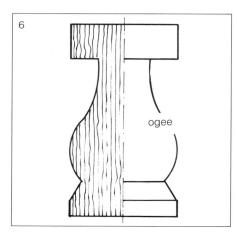

ogee

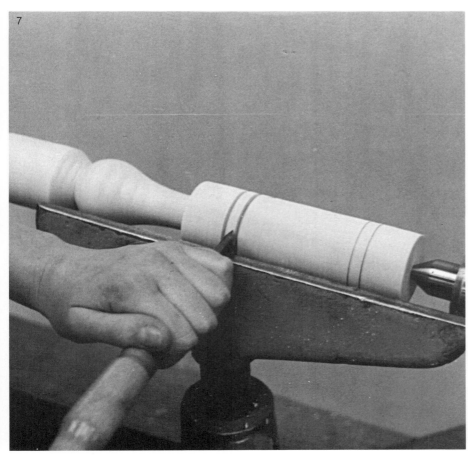

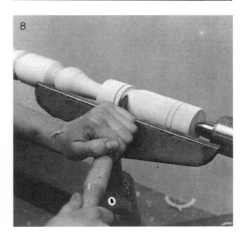

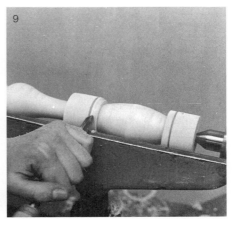

Turning bobbins is another variation of the long curve. The production of a bobbin between two beads is shown in Figs 7-9.

The markings are notched to the required depth into the workpiece using the tip of a skew. The bobbin is then turned. The waste wood is cut away from both sides, working from the centre outwards with a skew chisel. The beads are then shaped as required.

Fig 11 shows two turned bars which demonstrate the basic contours.

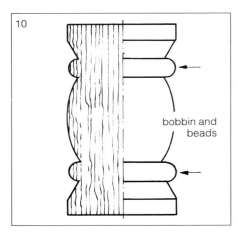

bobbin and beads

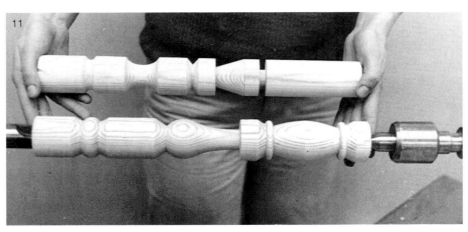

Faceplate turning is less common than spindle-turning. The grain runs at a right angle to the lathe axis, and the workpiece is fixed at only one end.

The wood is attached to a faceplate, or to a screw, cup or engineer's scroll chuck. The main work is done using a gouge, but skew chisels and scrapers are also used.

Hollowing is usually necessary on plates, bowls and jars. The hollows are turned using special scrapers. This requires most particular care.

The production of small batches of turned work is still done by hand, whereas large batches are machine produced. Templates and copying equipment are used to provide exact copies of the original.

Holes are bored with drills in either horizontal or vertical positions. Even if the workpieces are not very big, it is essential to mount them firmly.

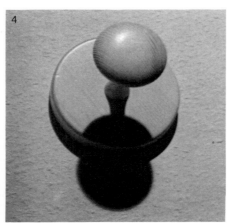

In faceplate turning the wood is mounted at one end only. The driving centre is replaced by a faceplate, by a screw, cup or engineer's scroll chuck.

The wood grain runs at a right angle to the lathe axis, i.e. the workpiece is mounted in the side grain. This means that the direction of the grain on the surface being worked is constantly changing. The tools cut into the wood along the grain as well as against it.

The blanks must always be well centred so that the lathe can turn smoothly and without vibration.
Large, heavy or unrounded parts must first be balanced out by being turned at a low speed and roughed down to a cylinder.

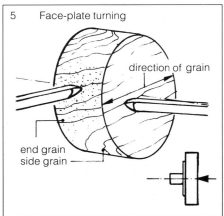

Fig 1 shows a piece of rough oak with its edges cut off. Before mounting on a screw chuck, a pilot hole of about 7-8 mm in diameter is bored. The run of the grain can be see clearly here.
Fig. 3 shows the roughing of a cylinder with a gouge, at about 800 rpm.

For a flush fit, e.g. on a faceplate, the side of the workpiece that is attached to the plate should first be levelled with a plane. In order to work the end grain surface, the tool rest must be swung round at 90° and pushed up to about 3 mm away from the wood.

Fig 2 shows a piece of rough cherrywood cut to a disc with a bandsaw and mounted on a faceplate. The diameter of the workpiece should be larger than that of the faceplate, so that the tool does not hit against it.

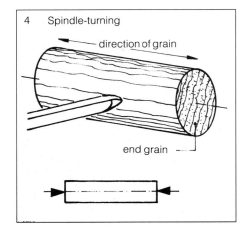

4 Spindle-turning

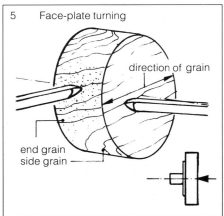

5 Face-plate turning

6

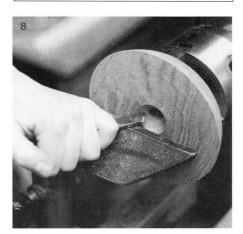

The tool is held to the left of the centre of rotation. This is the only position in which the blade can remove wood.
Fig 7 shows how the edge of a wooden disc is rounded with a gouge. This process is always worked from the centre outwards.

In Fig 8 the inside of a bowl is being turned: a cone-shaped hollow is being cut in the centre with a skew.
Fig 9 shows an example of cup chuck turning. A hollow cylinder is mounted on an engineer's scroll chuck and serviette rings are turned from it.

Fig 12: The use of copying equipment is possible in spindle as well as faceplate turning. Here the copying attachment has been swivelled at 90° to the lathe axis. The acrylic template can be seen clearly. The copying mechanism is operated by two handwheels.

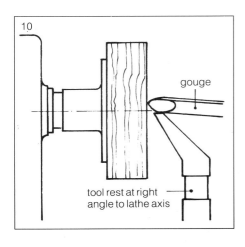

gouge

tool rest at right angle to lathe axis

6   Hollowing

from above

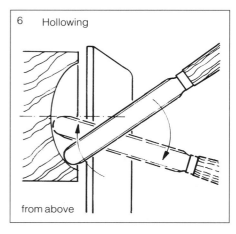

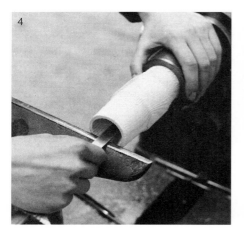

Figs 1-9 show how a small pinewood block is hollowed out. After the wood has been mounted on a screw chuck the gouge is moved from the outside to the centre with slightly increasing pressure. This process shaves off the wood little by little, in a ring pattern.

A slight elevation remains in the centre at first (see Fig 2).

Now the central elevation is removed (Fig 7). The gouge must be handled very carefully so that the turning motion does not cause it to stray too far to the right of the centre of rotation, where it could be grabbed, causing the blade to damage the inside surface.

The gouge is held on the tool rest with the left hand while the right hand moves the handle to the left. The edge of the tool rest is more or less the pivot for the gouge movement. The depth of the hollow is measured with a template or vernier callipers. Hollow turning is mainly used in the production of bowls, plates and jars.

Deeper recesses can be hollowed using a bent scraper. On these pages the process is shown using a gouge, however, as this is an easier tool for the amateur to handle.

Figs 10 and 11 illustrate how the depth of a hollow is measured. When working pieces are mounted on screw chucks it is particularly important not to hollow out so deeply that the tip of the screw shows through.

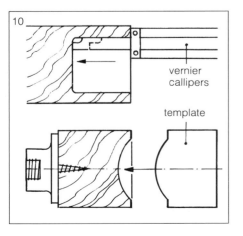

vernier callipers

template

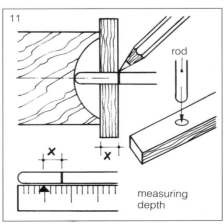

rod

measuring depth

Copy turning is recommended as a method for producing turnings with identical contours. A practical template, as is illustrated here, is made from cardboard. This ensures copies are identical. Copy turning may be done in either the spindle or the faceplate position.

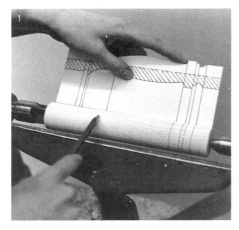

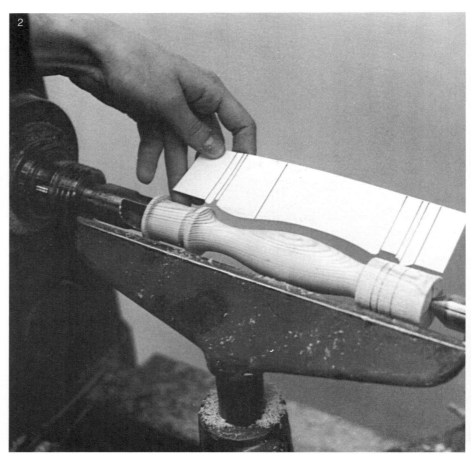

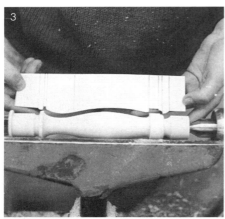

The template has two parts: a positive and a negative shape. Fig 1 shows the marking out of the contour points.
Fig 3 illustrates the use of the template more clearly. The blank is to be turned to fit into the shape of the template.

The negative shape of the template is held against the workpiece several times while it is being turned to check the accuracy of the shape. It should fit flush against the completed turning.

Figs 4 and 5 demonstrate how the thickness of the template contour is compared against the workpiece using vernier callipers.
Fig 6 shows the template parts alongside the completed workpiece.

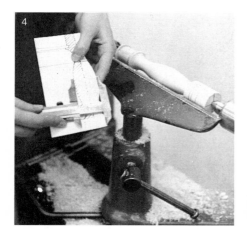

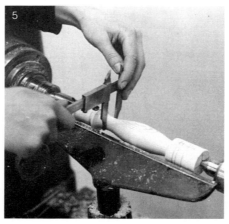

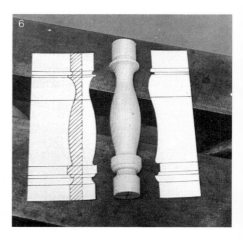

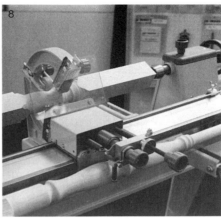

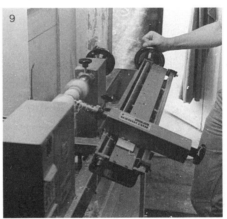

Copying equipment can be mounted on a lathe to turn such things as batches of table legs, knobs, spindles for stairways or chairs. The master workpiece is traced along its contours using a special mechanism. This is directly connected to a turning tool which makes the same motions as a hand-held tool and copies the contours on the blank.

With small machines the piece to be copied is halved and copied on an acrylic plate, which is then screwed to a bracket. The copying mechanism can be moved to and fro by turning a handwheel. There are special steels available for turning cylinders and simple contours, and pointed tools for sharply formed profiles as well as detailed work. These tools are made of high speed steel (HSS).

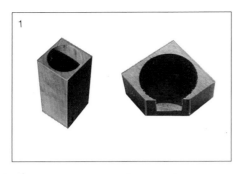

Drilling on a lathe is very easy and precise and, most importantly, can be done axially. The process is the reverse of using a drill, as the bit stays still while the workpiece rotates.

The bit is fixed in a drilling chuck mounted in the tailstock.

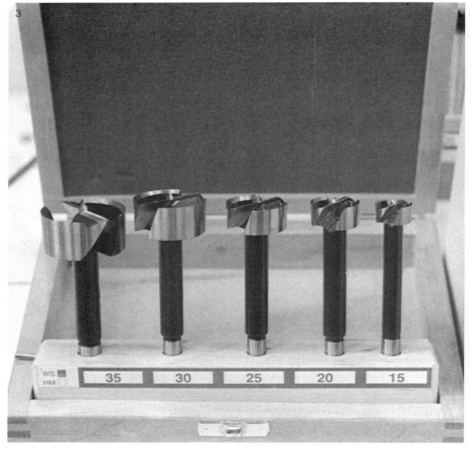

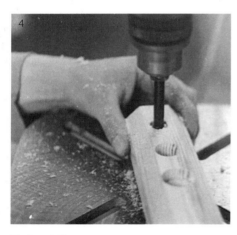

Twist drills are generally used to bore wide holes. They are spade-shaped in order to remove shavings better. They are not very suitable for boring deep holes.

Brad point drills usually have two cutters and bore very exactly.

Hole saws are used to bore wide holes. These are saw-like steel rings that may be interchanged according to the diameter required (up to 100 mm). The holes bored can only be as deep as the height of the ring. A drilling chuck's jaws extend from 1-16 mm. Boring should never be forced.

Forstner bits cut holes with very smooth sides. They are very good for hollowing out the flat bases of small jars as their cutters are not pointed. Only gentle pressure should be used with these.

Rasps tend to cut rather than bore into the wood. They consist of steel cylinders with narrow teeth on the sides.

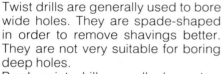

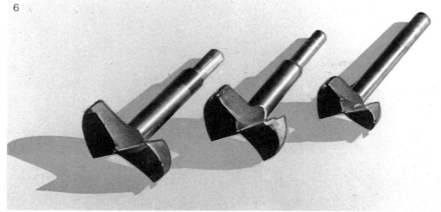

Eckhard Krummel, bowl made of Christ's thorn, 40 cm high, ⌀ 50 cm

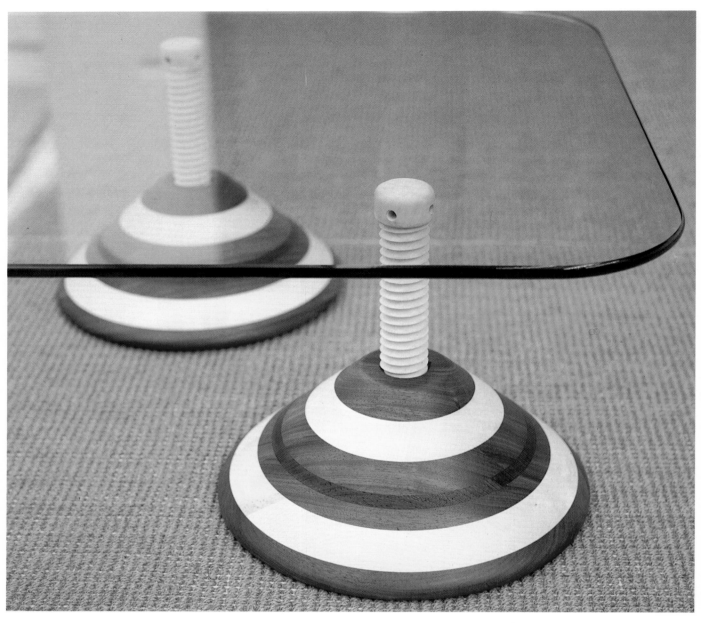

**Above and below: Waldemar Rothe, tables
from the collection *Wooden Art*
Wood used: padouk, millettia laurentii, maple
Production: C.A. Scheffler & Co., Switzerland**

While it is being bored, the workpiece is mounted on the lathe in either a cup of an engineer's scroll chuck. When the workpiece rotates, the bit is bored into it by turning the handwheel on the tailstock. Deep holes should not be bored all at once. The bit needs to be removed from the workpiece several times in order to remove shavings.

7

8

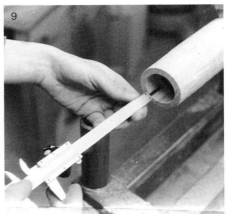

9

10

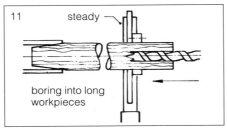

11
steady

boring into long workpieces

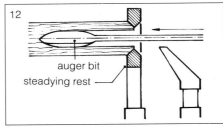

12
auger bit
steadying rest

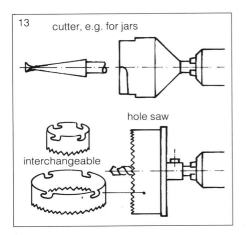

13
cutter, e.g. for jars

hole saw

interchangeable

14

Auger bits can be used to bore very long holes. They have a single cutter and are self-centring. Care must be taken to use straight-grained wood. The shavings are cut off spirally. A steadying rest can be fixed to the face of the workpiece. This is an iron ring which slants towards the centre and supports the workpiece. Working with an auger is something best left to the professional, however.

A steady is used to support long workpieces. As a rule it has three adjustable guide rollers, in which the cylindrical blank rotates.

Design

'Design is the art of creating usefulness and pleasure.' This was one of the doctrines of Vitruvius, the Roman architect famous at the time of Caesar Augustus.

Design cannot be forced into artificial rules, but it does follow laws of its own. The rule of the 'golden section' still holds, but from time to time it becomes unfashionable. Even the theory that a true master can be recognised by the restrictions he sets himself can be contradicted to a certain extent. In the USA the current trend is to replace the phrase 'less is more' by 'less is bore'.

In any case, design is something that cannot be created rationally. Emotion has just as great a role to play as calculation when talking about real creativity. Contrasts in expression, deviations from the norm and disharmony all create tension and so contribute to the character of an object.

Design planned before turning can involve various methods of laminating and design after turning, or methods of two- or three-dimensional surface enrichment. Changes in the shape of turned work, e.g. by carving and filing, can improve the appearance of the finished product.

Often the functional value of a turning and the value of experience behind it are realised only when the work is cut apart or has segments cut out of it. Surface enrichment plays an important part in design. It begins with sanding. The off-the-tool finish may include further treatment with transparent varnish or coloured lacquer, staining or painting.

Specialised turning techniques are best left to the master craftsman. They include ways of turning bent or twisted columns and cutting threads. Angular, oval, square-cut and eccentric turning also possible. Other techniques are also used, including the production of non-turned round and curved parts. These techniques really belong to the field of the joiner, but they have been mentioned here because their use sometimes makes more sense than ordinary turning.

Anyone who wants to be creative must set reason aside for a while and rely instead on his powers of intuition and his emotions. He must concentrate non-rationally on the object he intends to create. Only then can ideas emerge from his subconscious and develop into a more concrete form.

By combining a mind open to even rather unusual ideas, the acceptance of the strength coming from within, and the technical facilities available, a genuine work of art may be created.

Pleasure in experimenting, which presupposes a pleasure in the unexpected, is a basic requirement for real creativity. Living things cannot flourish in a dry, sterile atmosphere.

It is possible for design to be made systematically, following a strict framework of basic rules, but then there is a danger of creating series of monotonous shapes which appear tiring, boring and irritating because of their lack of imagination.

Art itself is not something which can be learned, which would lead to imposition of rules and so to imitations. However, an artistic *attitude* can be learned by stimulating sensual and conceptual perception and thus extending productive capability. For this, the study of nature and critical examination of works of art are absolutely essential.

The desire to express must be accompanied by a good measure of artistic understanding, and combined with the established rules of design in order to produce an object that is convincing – in either its originality or its conservatism – and that also takes contemporary taste into account. Even something extravagant can be thoroughly acceptable and stimulating as long as it does not offend the natural sense of form.

Naturally, some standards do exist, such as the golden section mentioned earlier, the laws of symmetry and other principles of design. These are guidelines even for people with talent, and enable ideas and plans to be tested in the light of general rules. As well as being harmonious, design can be loud and provacative, but even such restlessness seeks to conform to the written and unwritten rules of art.

'Aesthetics is the yardstick with which the culture of a society is measured.' Aesthetics is not a superstructure built high above necessity, nor is it simply an ingredient added to an otherwise empty existence. It is a way of giving structure to the cycle of life. Man's existence receives a valuable contribution from the style of the environment which he has created for himself.

Man lives and marvels. He expresses himself in words, gestures, pictures and constructed shapes.

Shape cannot be observed in isolation, but only within a special structure, a framework. Shape is not arbitrary; it is symbolic and significant, an element of the life force. The function of shape is to give to content both visual reality and the ability to be experienced. Its criteria are usefulness and originality.

Today, formal aspects are being re-examined. We have learned a lot from the failure of modern architecture to satisfy demands made by emotions. It is important to us to unite the functional with the emotional and so to create a worthwhile quality. Emotion is not satisfied by just the practical and the pragmatic. It requires the addition of intellectual components, a spiritualised synopsis and adequate expression.

Spiritual health means not only a logical comprehension of the world, but an inner commitment when dealing with the things connected to the world. Commitment finds its basis in personal environments. Man wants to feel at home in the world and to furnish his own environment, i.e. to surround himself with objects whose shape and characteristics suit him. Only thus is it possible to discover his identity. In the living area, the smallest private unit, the task of design therefore has great significance.

Creativity is psychic in nature and is of inestimable value in the realisation of personality. Creativity can itself create a sense of achievement. Talent, the will to work and sound theoretical knowledge are combined with temperament, daring and the desire for success.

Active creativity is a dialectical relationship between thinking, planning and achievement on the one hand and profound emotional fulfilment on the other.

There are three reasons for producing or designing an object: usefulness, the enjoyment of beautiful things and the pleasure of working. Strength of craftsmanship lies in the unity found when the hand that creates the design also performs the work.

The first step, that of setting the aim of the work, is followed by the operational phase – the transfer of the plan into clear definitions of material, size and structure. The plan gains shape; work can then begin.

'Ornare' is the Latin word meaning 'to adorn' – an original form of human expression. Ornamentation is essentially enrichment by adornment, construction and emphasis. The basic shape of an object is formed first of all, but it is then improved and interpreted by ornamentation. Excessive ornament is to be avoided as much as too little.

The spiritual value of an object is closely related to its functional use, which it elevates to a higher and more significant plane. The shape becomes the bearer of design. The idea and the material cannot be separated, but must suit and complement each other.

The fact that decoration is always determined by the material should never be forgotten. Falsifications arise from over-emphasis of the statements made by the material itself, which must be avoided. This is particularly important when using wood which is itself strongly expressive. Ornamentation should not compete with the material used. Distinctive grain, for example, precludes the excessive shaping of contours.

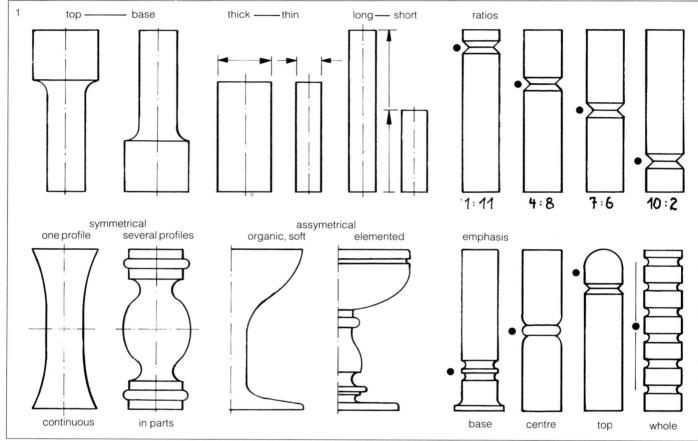

1 top ——— base   thick ——— thin   long — short   ratios
1:11   4:8   7:6   10:2

symmetrical
one profile   several profiles
continuous   in parts

assymetrical
organic, soft   elemented

emphasis
base   centre   top   whole

Ornamentation has its origin in technological and functional circumstances which arose from the ways in which objects and building components had to be manufactured, resulting possibly from the production of grooves, holes, rings in tools, casts of mounts or construction joints. Thus ornamentation does not have its origin in decoration for its own sake.

The setting of accents through detail in design must be spontaneous and not too complicated; it should not appear deliberate. Emphasis and accentuation are effective measures to combat monotony. When it is emphasised, an object acquires a 'face' with which it can communicate. It is through this communication that we can really use and benefit from the object.

Harmony or contrast emerge from the movement and countermovement of round and square, of convex and concave shapes, from keeping to normal proportions on the one hand or exaggerating them on the other. Balance or tension is justified by the object of the design in the form of harmony or challenge.

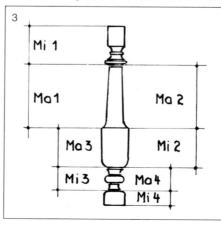

2 Golden Section construction

$BD \cdot \frac{1}{2} AB$

$\frac{AB}{2}$

A   C   B
Ma   Mi
Major   Minor

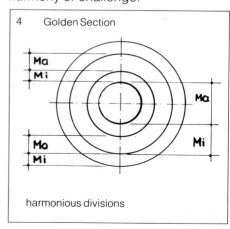

3
Mi 1
Ma 1   Ma 2
Ma 3   Mi 2
Mi 3   Ma 4
Mi 4

4 Golden Section
Ma
Mi
Ma
Mi
Ma
Mi
Mi
harmonious divisions

The necessary proportions of objects determine their outward appearance. In the case of small everyday articles the way they fit in the hand is important; with furniture and building components, it is the measurements of the human body. The feel and scale of an object are important criteria to consider when creating the design. The rhythm of the interplay of forces in the flow of shapes materialises when joints, distances, repetitions, juxtapositions and oppositions are combined with due consideration.

A dynamic force emerges from the interplay between strong and weak profiling. The change from wide to slender or from much to little profiling directs the eye towards the basic energetic strength of being alive.

Rules

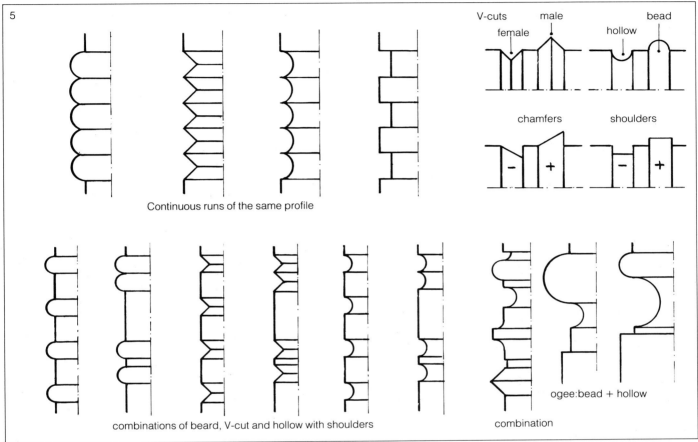

Continuous runs of the same profile

combinations of beard, V-cut and hollow with shoulders

combination

ogee:bead + hollow

The dimensions of an object influence the extent to which it can be decorated. Decoration should be placed in positions which offer the best visual and structural possibilities and give the optimum effect. Decoration cannot be treated randomly. The height, length, width and diameter of an object determine the allocation of its decoration.

The various contours that woodturning offers the designer have already been dealt with. Their use is left to individual taste. Depending on the woodturner's skill, in his hands they will become a willing, expressive form of design. But the choice of contour made will depend on the object to be produced.

The artistic unity of shape of a piece of work is the result of correctly-understood rules and a personal ability to understand the nature of the object. The entire form must be self-explanatory. Where a living shape has been created, any commentary is superfluous. Only when nothing more can be interpreted into it and nothing can be added to improve it has the limit of a design been reached.

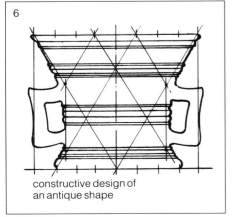

constructive design of an antique shape

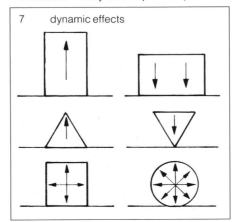

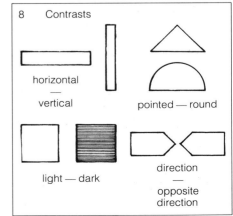

Wood is laminated for technical as well as for design reasons. Side-grain laminating can be done by simply gluing pieces of wood together (i.e. without use of special wood joints). Solid wood is cut up and glued together again to remove internal stress.

Seen creatively, laminating is a very variable process. However, it has to suit the technical conditions of the material and take into account the swelling and shrinkage of wood.

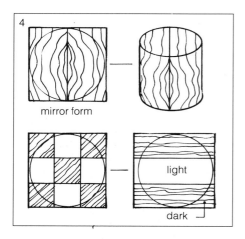

Strictly speaking, laminating of cross-cut wood is not at all durable without using wood joints. Usually special joints are needed to glue short pieces of wood together. Comb joints, shown in Fig 6, are excellent for this purpose.

But lamination is not usually done, for economic reasons. When it is used, it is done in such a way that wastage is greatly reduced — for example, the foot of a lamp stand or a table leg is blocked all around, but only in the places that jut out.

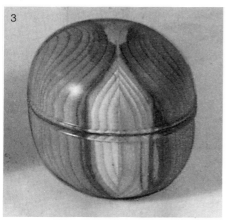

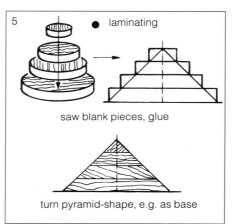

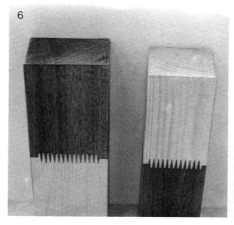

Similar and dissimilar wood types may be laminated, in either parallel or mirrored arrangements. In this way contrast and harmony in colour and shape may be achieved. Side and end-grain structures may be featured effectively, as may heart and sapwood, annual rings and medullary rays.

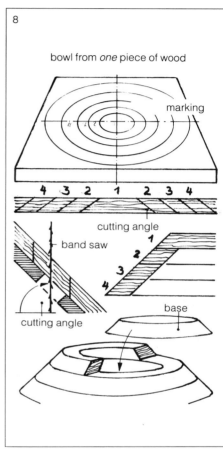

bowl from *one* piece of wood

marking

cutting angle

band saw

cutting angle

base

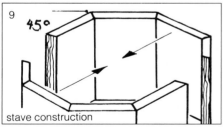

45°

stave construction

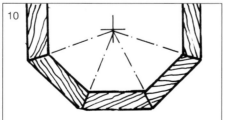

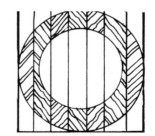

Surface enrichment of turnings may be either two or three-dimensional. Poker-work is the oldest and most common method of decorating turned work. This involves singeing or lightly charring the wood using suitable tools.

Surface enrichment – 2-dimensional

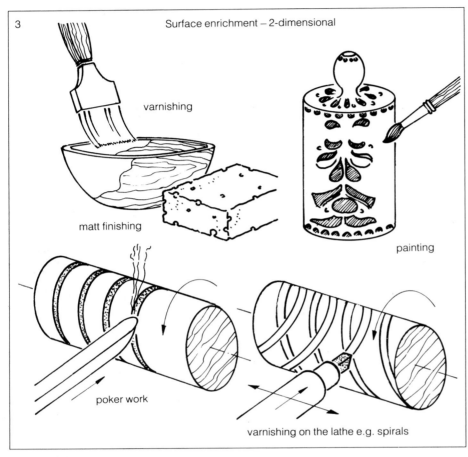

varnishing

matt finishing

painting

poker work

varnishing on the lathe e.g. spirals

Surface enrichment – 3-dimensional

fluting

cut or carved after turning

Staining and dyeing, matt finishing and varnishing, painting and spraying are done by a turner in exactly the same way as by a joiner.
A coat of paint covers up the wood's natural grain, so that the overall shape becomes more apparent. No matter how beautiful the grain of the wood may be, it will still compete with the turned contours.

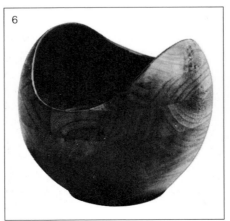

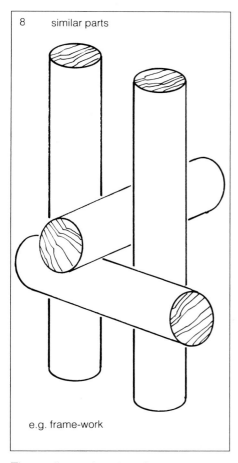

8 similar parts

e.g. frame-work

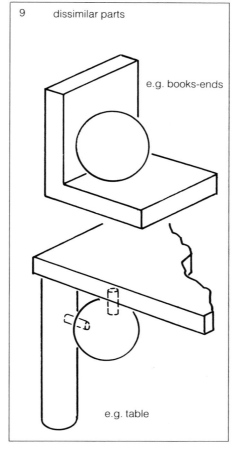

9 dissimilar parts

e.g. books-ends

e.g. table

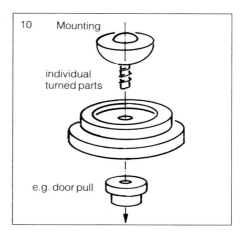

10 Mounting

individual turned parts

e.g. door pull

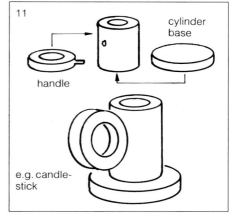

11

cylinder base

handle

e.g. candle-stick

Three-dimensional surface treatment after turning takes many forms, and is demonstrated in Figs 5-7, and Figs 12-14. Simply cutting wood away is particularly easy. Making curves by filing or sanding is more difficult. Carving has the greatest effect.

The combination of different turned parts with each other, or even with unturned wood, creates very effective designs, as Figs 8-11 show.

12

13

14

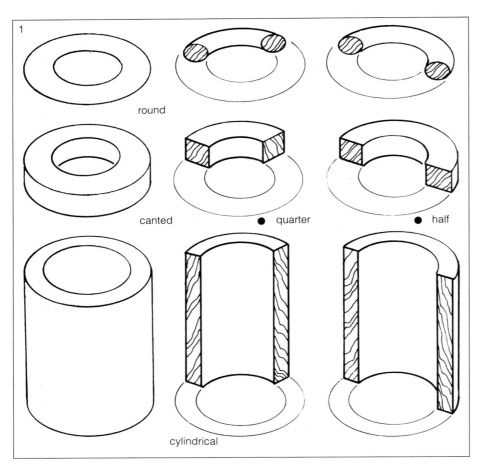

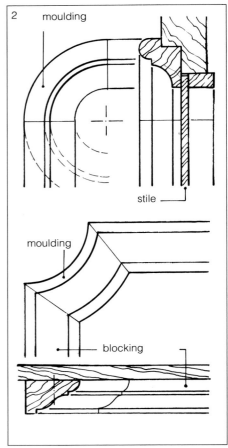

round

canted   ● quarter   ● half

cylindrical

The cutting out of square-edged or rounded, turned rings into quarter of half circles (shown in abstract form in Fig 1) gives an awareness of how widely this method has always been used.

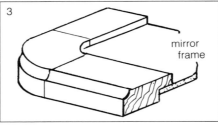

mirror frame

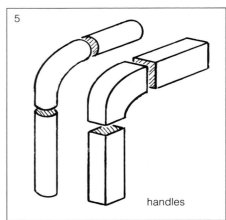

moulding

stile

moulding

blocking

Moulding, blocking and stiles between panels, for example, can decorate cupboard doors or serve as frames. Very often the frames are decorated with corners that curve inward or outward. Another way of putting the work to use is to make various types of handle.

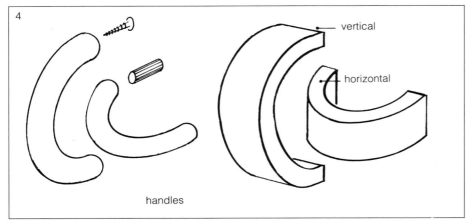

vertical

horizontal

handles

handles

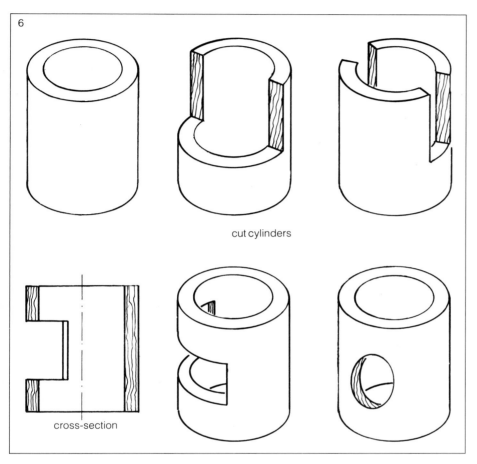

cut cylinders

cross-section

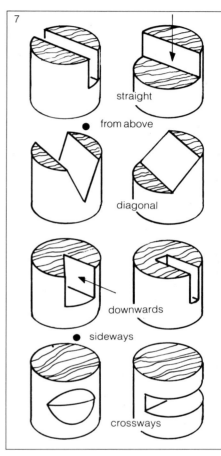

straight

from above

diagonal

downwards

sideways

crossways

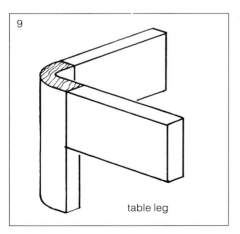

Offsetting cylinders or bars, or cutting or boring into them either at the side or on top, offers further technical and creative possibilities. In this way containers are given handles, the body of an object is given edges, tables and beds are given legs. Even

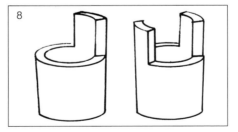

shelves and door-frames can be fitted into the spaces obtained by cutting wood away.

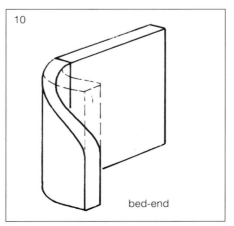

table leg

bed-end

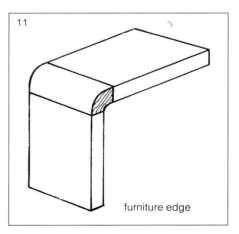

furniture edge

Cutting solid or hollow turned work apart changes its appearance remarkably. The abstract confrontation of discs, cylinders, spheres and pyramids cut in half or quarters gives a good outline of the various uses possible.

This form of off-the-tool treatment has been used since ancient times.

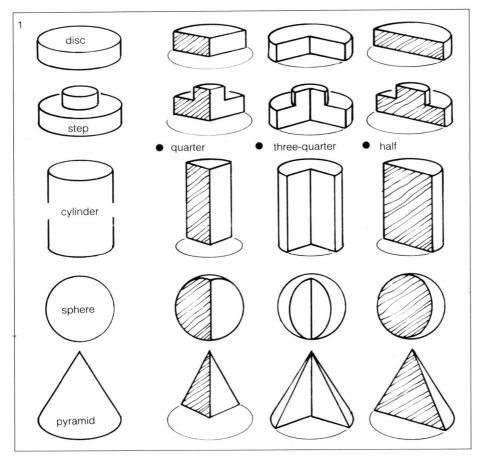

1

disc

step

● quarter ● three-quarter ● half

cylinder

sphere

pyramid

2

e.g. split knobs

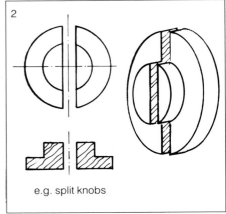

3

e.g. staggered posts

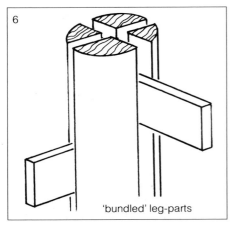

4

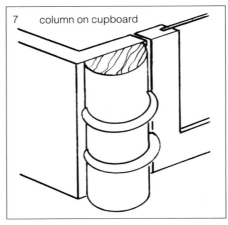

6

'bundled' leg-parts

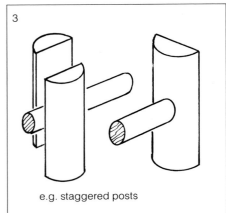

7 column on cupboard

5

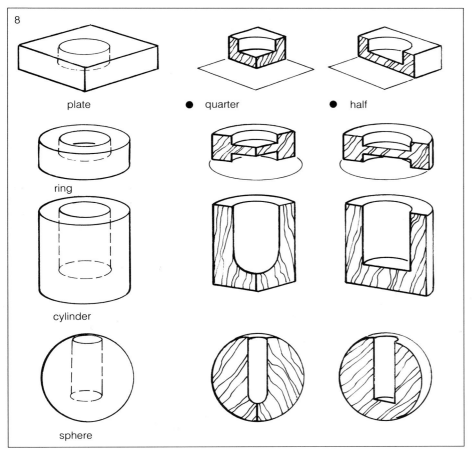

8

plate ● quarter ● half

ring

cylinder

sphere

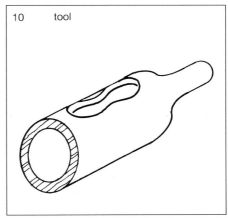

9

door pull

10   tool

Examples of ornamental columns on cupboards, door-pulls, tools, flour scoops etc can all be found.

Even our own time finds a means of expression in the creation of these objects, as in table frames, for example (see pp. 80-1).

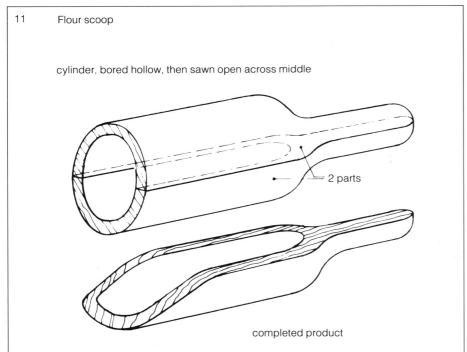

11   Flour scoop

cylinder, bored hollow, then sawn open across middle

2 parts

completed product

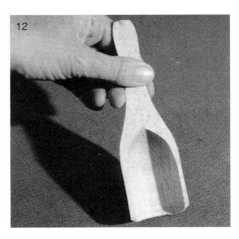

12

Changing turned work by splitting it or cutting it apart is a tremendously exciting aspect of creativity, particularly when various combinations can then be experimented with and assembled.

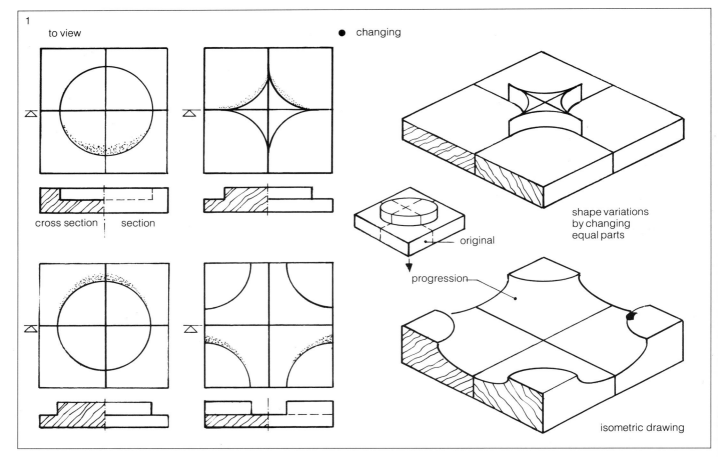

shape variations by changing equal parts

isometric drawing

When axially symmetrical squares with a turned surface are fixed together in a new combination, a completely different surface decoration results (Fig 1). The combination of circular shapes with pieces removed produces new figures (Fig 3). Cutting up and changing the parts of richly ornamented cylinders emphasises their profiling (Fig 4).

Halved table legs with the cut surface turned outwards are very effective. The break in anticipation that this causes lends the table a progressive nuance.

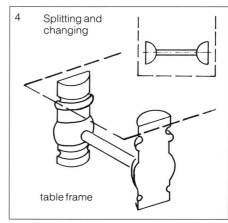

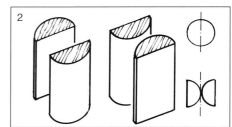

putting together

adding

coupling

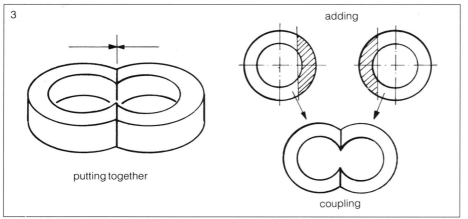

Splitting and changing

table frame

Karl Kremel, (above) double-lidded jar, cherry
(below) bowl made of untreated walnut

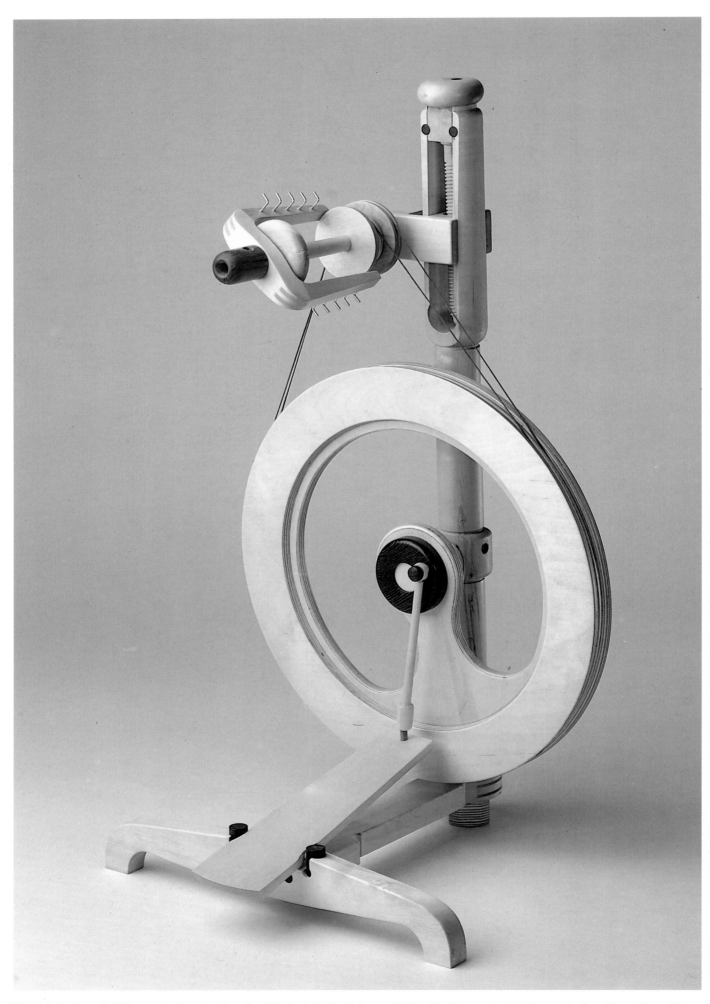

Heinrich Andreas Schilling, spinning-wheel made of birch and millettia laurentii, 50 x 50 x 95 cm, wheel ∅ 48 cm, spindle ∅ 13 mm, Two-string drive, hackle and bobbin may be changed without removing the driving string from the wheel

Staggering parts and twisting them sideways, upwards or spirally is shown in abstract in Figs 5 and 6, and in practice in Figs 10 and 11 in the cupboard columns and the lampstand made of discs of various diameters.

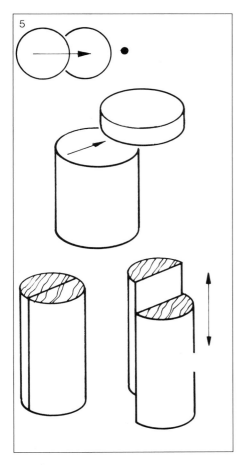

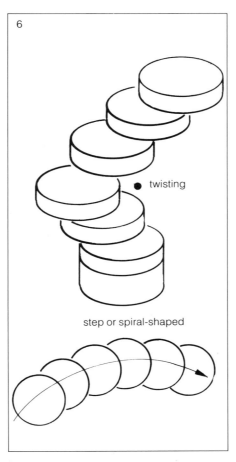

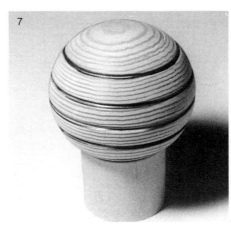

twisting

step or spiral-shaped

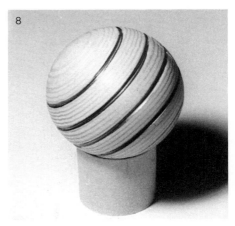

The tilting of a wooden ball only shows up effectively when a profile has been cut into the surface. Stair-posts often used to be decorated with such emphatic knobs (Figs 9 and 12).

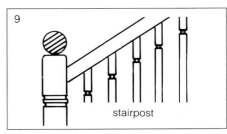

stairpost

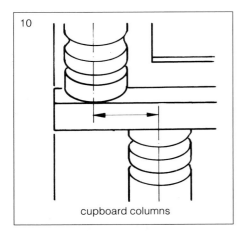

cupboard columns

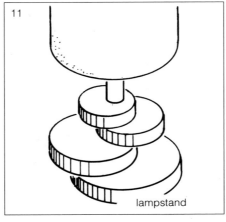

lampstand

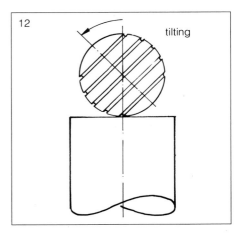

tilting

Dividing turnings and then combining the new shapes offers an amazingly varied means of creativity. The possibilities it provides should be brought to mind again and again when seeking new ways of making statements.

The design of bannisters has always been made with great care. The design of the spaces between the cylindrical bars deserves at least as much attention as that of the contours themselves.

The contours of boards, e.g. of a balcony balustrade, show the effect of the alternation between surface and and space particularly well.

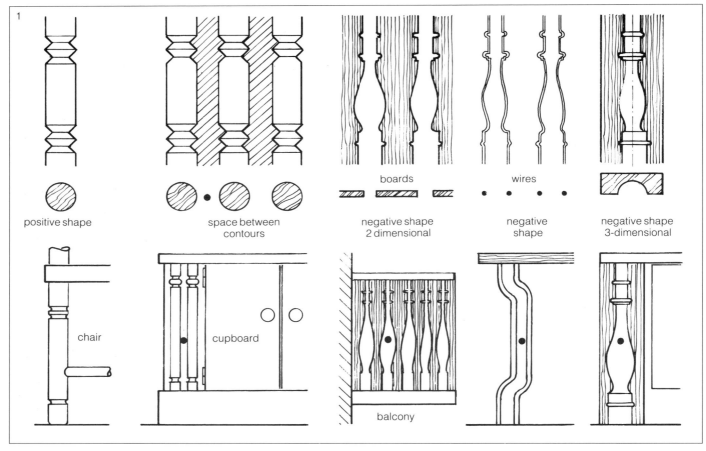

Copying the silhouettes of posts in wire leads to an interesting way around the so-called 'positive' and 'negative' shapes.

The spaces between the contours provide the counterpart to halved columns (see Fig 4). They are a popular element in modern design, even in building construction.

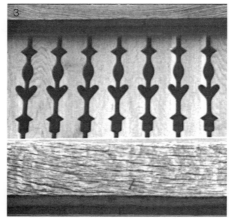

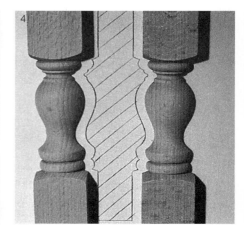

The contours of a column become particularly well defined when a slot is cut into it. A crack in a column, caused by faulty drying, illustrates this clearly. The connection of the column to another surface, e.g. by means of a slot, is useful from the point of view of design, as well as being technically convenient:

Negative shapes become apparent at the ends of profiles. Using this to advantage with crosspieces and borings, the placing of positive and negative shapes, or even pushing them one inside the other deserves attention.

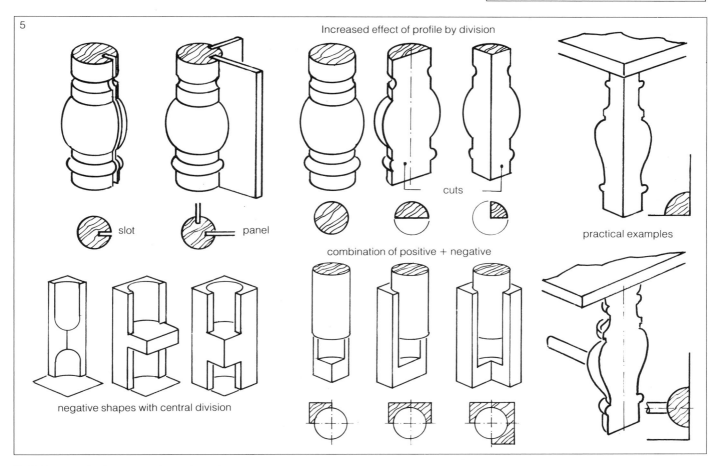

5

Increased effect of profile by division

slot

panel

cuts

combination of positive + negative

practical examples

negative shapes with central division

Splitting workpieces and turning the parts around results in intervals between the contours, as illustrated in Fig 8.

6

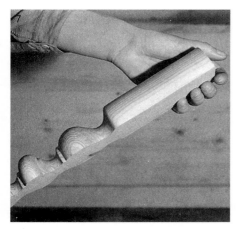

7

8

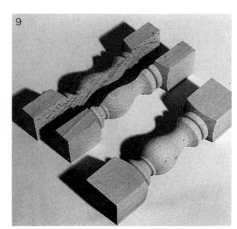

9

After a workpiece has been turned, it must be sanded. Only slight sanding will be necessary if the wood has been turned cleanly. Sanding will smooth the wood's surface.

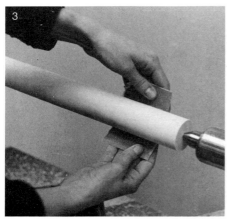

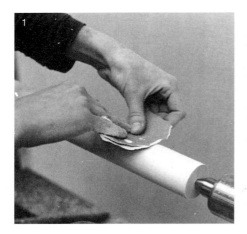

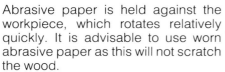

Abrasive paper is held against the workpiece, which rotates relatively quickly. It is advisable to use worn abrasive paper as this will not scratch the wood.

Three grit grades will usually suffice: 80 or 100 for preliminary rough sanding, 150 for the second and 280 for the final sanding.

The tool rest should be removed before sanding, otherwise it will be in the way and the turner's fingers could be trapped between the workpiece and the tool rest. Figs 1-10 demonstrate the correct method of holding the paper. The speed of the lathe may be increased; moving abrasive paper along the workpiece requires very little strength.

For sanding fine hollows, the abrasive paper can first be bent around a rod (Fig 2). On straight surfaces it is held flat (Figs 1, 3 and 9). For sanding bowls the paper is folded in two and held against the sides (Fig 4). The paper should not be too large, otherwise it will not fit properly up against the shape.

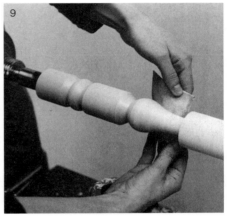

A polishing wheel may be mounted on the lathe in place of the workpiece, in which case the pieces to be sanded need only be held up against it.

A sanding block made from a piece of cork can be used for some work. A very even surface can be achieved with this on e.g. a cylindrical post.

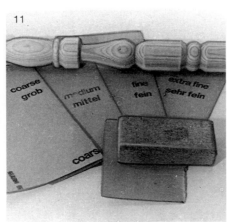

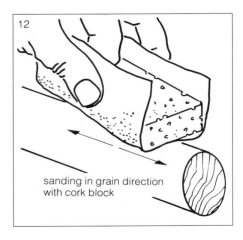

sanding in grain direction with cork block

Finishing of the surface of workpieces follows immediately after sanding on the lathe. The wood is rubbed with shavings, which gives a very smooth surface (see Fig 1). A strip of leather has the same effect.

Spraying It is essential to ensure there is sufficient ventilation when using a spray gun. It is best to spray out of doors, with the air as free of dust as possible. First the varnish must be thinned (10-50%) and well stirred. It should not be thinned too little (which will mean no vaporisation or too coarse a finish) or too much (as varnish runs, leaves streaks, and has poor covering power).

When the operating lever of the spray gun is pressed, varnish is sucked in, mixed with the compressed air and then vaporised through the jet. The advantage is very neat results. The disadvantage is that this method is expensive.

The thinning proportions and the drying time are usually recommended by the manufacturer. Before varnishing the workpiece, it is best to practise on a piece of waste material.

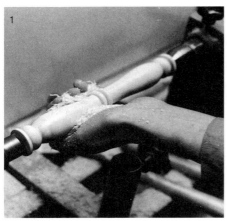

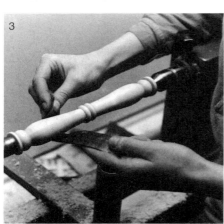

The spray gun should be held at a distance of 15-30 cm from the workpiece and pointed away from it when switched on, so that it is not hit by the first surge of varnish. Several thin coats of varnish are better than one thick coat.

Finishing with a piece of soapstone is very easy, and effective, giving the surface a silky gloss (see Fig 2).

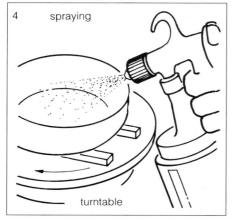

4 spraying

turntable

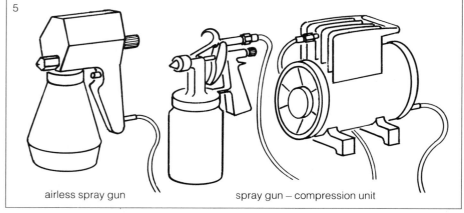

5

airless spray gun

spray gun – compression unit

Bowls, jars and plates are put on a turntable before spraying. The spray gun must be held steady and tilted only slightly. Care must be taken that no streaks of varnish form on the inside.

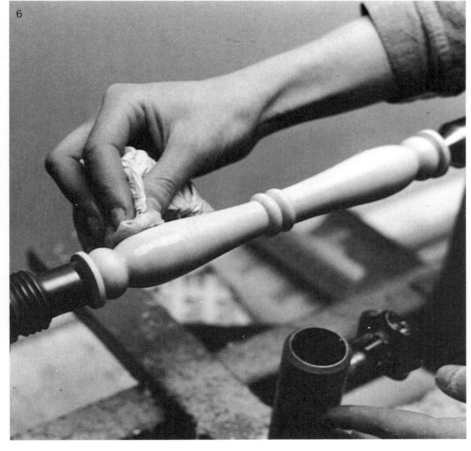

Wood can be impregnated using a soft cloth, and should be rubbed with a dry cloth or with soft, clean paper afterwards (Fig 6).

Fig 7: The foot of a piece of furniture is being stained using a soft-bristled brush. Shortly after the staining liquid has been absorbed, a dry brush is used to remove any excess. The brush should be moved in the direction of the grain.

Fig 10: A serviette ring is being rubbed with wood-oil while mounted on a homemade spigot chuck.

Fig 8: A small, turned ring is being dipped into a plastic bowl of staining liquid. After dipping, the rings are hung on a line to dry. Hanging up rings is recommended after varnishing (Fig 11).

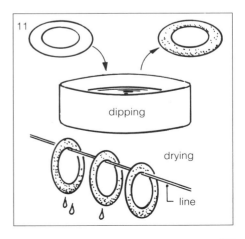

The treatment or finishing of the surface of the wood is often necessary for technical as well as for artistic reasons. A protective coat of varnish or other treatment prevents dust from getting into the pores, makes the wood resistant to damp and general wear through everyday use, and increases its durability.

Ornamental design often means objects are decorated extremely richly; to a large extent the turned work is very often covered up by this. Varnish and paint are available in a variety of tones, consistencies and sizes. Those in screw-topped bottles are more practical but also more expensive than those in tins with push-on lids.

An improvement in the visual effect of the wood grain, its natural tone or the emphatically worked out appearance of the workpiece results.

Mixing various shades together is an inviting idea, but you must first consider how the products will react with one another.

Staining Staining gives wood a transparent colour which accentuates the grain. The staining liquid itself has no protective function, and therefore a protective finish must be applied afterwards.

Staining liquid may be bought ready for use in various shades. It can also be bought in dry form and made up later.

Before staining the turning, it is best to give a piece of waste wood a trial stain and let it dry, to judge the result. The liquid should be applied steadily with a soft, flat brush or a sponge. It must be left for a short while to take effect, and then the excess removed with a dry brush.

Straining liquid should only be put into plastic or enamel containers, never metal pots!

Priming Priming supplies the undercoat to a protective coat on a stained or untreated surface. It closes the pores of the wood and creates a connection between the wood and its protective coating. The primer is applied with a soft, flat brush. It dries in about 30 minutes and must then be sanded with 280 grit abrasive paper.

Varnishing Varnishing provides the wood with a clear, transparent, glossy coat of excellent durability. It seals the surface.

A distinction is made between varnish made of synthetic resin and that made of nitrocellulose. In both cases the work must first be primed.

The varnish is applied with a flat brush and should be left to dry for several hours. As a rule two coats should be sufficient. Varnish may be diluted with a special thinner (observe the manufacturer's instructions).

Matt finish A matt finish gives the wood a silk-like, glossy protective coating. Nitrocellulose or shellac are used as the binding agent. There are three possible methods of application. First a piece of cotton-knit cloth is formed into a ball which is held in the hand. The matt coat is applied sparingly, using only slight pressure on the cloth, which should not be too wet. This is enough to create a pleasant effect. A soft, flat brush can also be used for the same job, particularly when the turning has a complicated shape with hollows which the cotton wad cannot reach. A spray gun gives very even treatment. Guns working with either high or low pressure can be used.

Oiling Oiling (with linseed oil) enlivens the structure of the wood. It is normally used on tropical varieties of wood, such as teak, pitchpine or mahogany, which contain a certain type of resin which prevents varnishes from drying.

The workpiece is oiled using a cloth while it is still on the moving lathe. Small workpieces are dipped in the oil.

Wood absorbs oils well. Oil is water-repellent, respires and is obtained naturally. Once it is dry the surface needs to be polished.

Polishing When the workpiece has been given a matt finish, waxed or oiled, the finishing process is concluded by polishing. It is usually enough to rub the workpiece with a wad of cotton or cotton-wool while it is still rotating on the lathe. The longer the polishing process takes, the higher the gloss will be!

Waxing Waxing is popular for giving an antique effect. A solution of beeswax is used. Preparation before waxing need be no more than sanding with 220 grit paper. The wax is applied with a wad of cotton. It must be allowed to dry overnight and subsequently smoothed with a horse-hair brush.

Beeswax is neither water nor alcohol-proof.

Spraying Spraying an object results in a very even surface and means a shorter drying time. However, more equipment is required, as well as considerable skill. Airless spray guns and guns with compressors are available. The airless guns are simple and reasonably priced; they work with a piston pump which sucks in the varnish and sprays it out through a jet. The disadvantages of these are: low performance; the varnish must be heavily diluted; and the loud rattling of the pump.

High-pressure spray guns consist of an air-compressor, often with a separate pressure pot, and the spray gun.

All of these special techniques are reserved first and foremost for the professional turner. They are mentioned here only to give the amateur an idea of the potential diversity of woodturning. Further details are very seldom found, even in specialised literature.

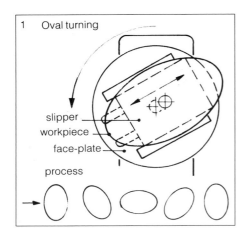

1 Oval turning

slipper
workpiece
face-plate

process

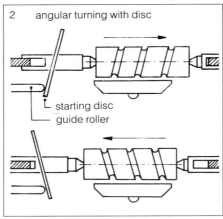

2 angular turning with disc

starting disc
guide roller

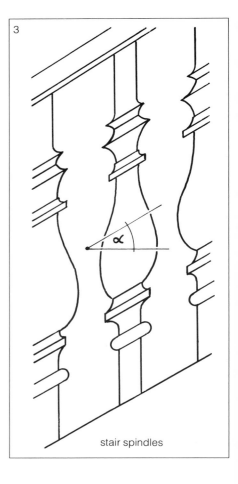

3

stair spindles

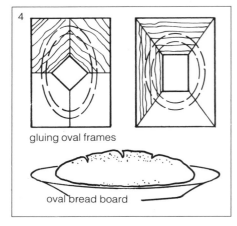

4

gluing oval frames

oval bread board

5 angular turning, longitudinal

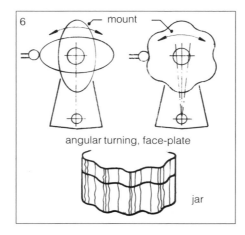

various angles

Oval pieces are turned with the aid of a special mount which is fitted on the lathe. The workpiece is moved diagonally back and forth. For this, a slipper is specially mounted on a faceplate.

The wood for oval picture frames must be carefully glued together before marking, cutting out and turning. Fig 4 illustrates how the pieces of wood can be arranged with regard to the run of the grain.

The technique of turning oval shapes is attractive, but nowadays it has been almost completely replaced by spindle moulding.

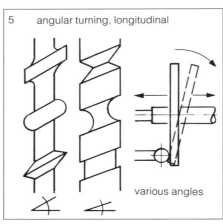

6 mount

angular turning, face-plate

jar

Angular turning is practised with the aid of a cross support. The lathe is changed into a kind of copying machine. A starting disc holds the guide roller. Angular turning makes possible the horizontal contouring of sloping posts. Thus a sloping table leg has its contours cut not at right angles to its centre axis, but, rather, parallel to the table top. Any angle may be chosen and angular turning may be done either parallel or at right angles to the lathe axis.

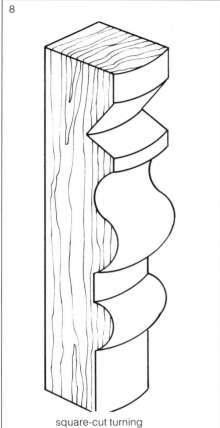

8

square-cut turning

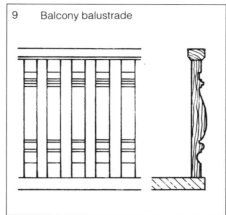

9 Balcony balustrade

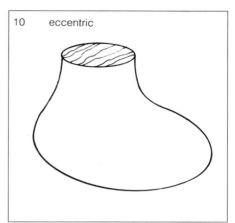

10 eccentric

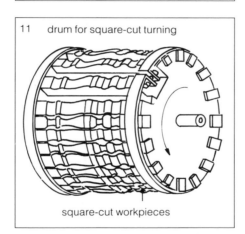

11 drum for square-cut turning

square-cut workpieces

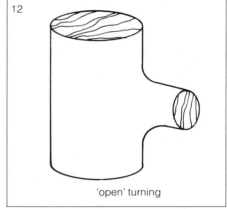

12

'open' turning

Turning contours into a series of square-cut pieces of wood is done using a drum on which each piece is mounted individually. Large series of balcony balustrades are turned in this way (see Figs 7-9, 11).

Turning eccentrically is quite possible for the professional woodturner, as is 'open' turning, in which one area is omitted during the turning process while the rest of the workpiece is turned normally. This is used, for example, where particular shaping of the wood is necessary for joining to another piece, such as the joint of a chair back.

13

Special techniques have been developed to satisfy particular functional and creative demands. A chair leg must be turned, for example, so that it can still serve as the support for the sloping chair back.

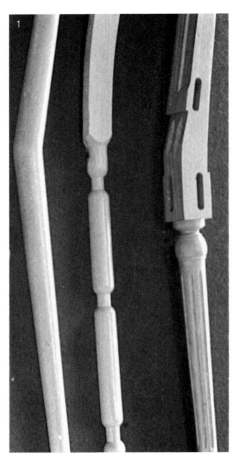

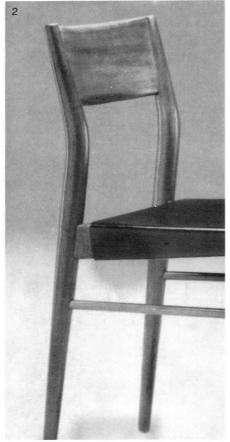

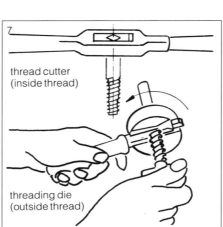

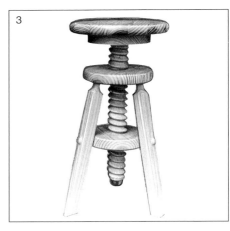

A twisted column can be turned so that it is oval in its cross-section.
Bent columns can be turned fairly easily using discs or special clamps, which need to be re-set several times.

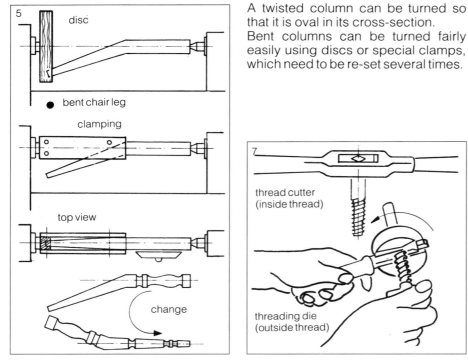

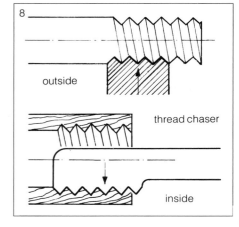

Threads can be cut by hand using a threading die, or turned on the lathe using a special thread chaser.
Today twisted columns, which were once chiselled, rasped and filed by hand, are machine-moulded.

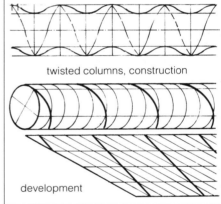

twisted columns, construction

development

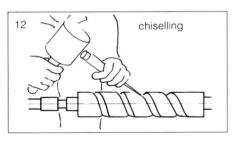

chiselling

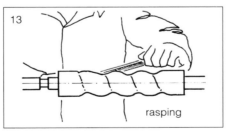

rasping

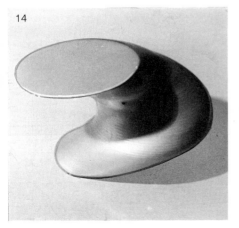

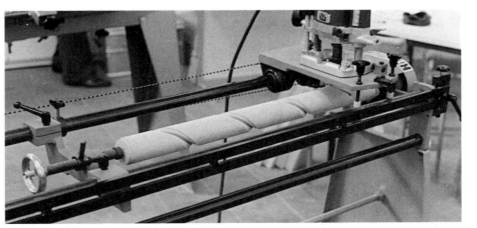

Joiners have at their disposal many possibilities for forming round or curved parts. Wood may be cut to a round or curved shape, bent, or laminated in layers or blocks.
Routing, boring and copying are very economical processes.

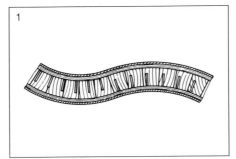

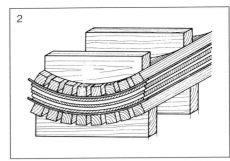

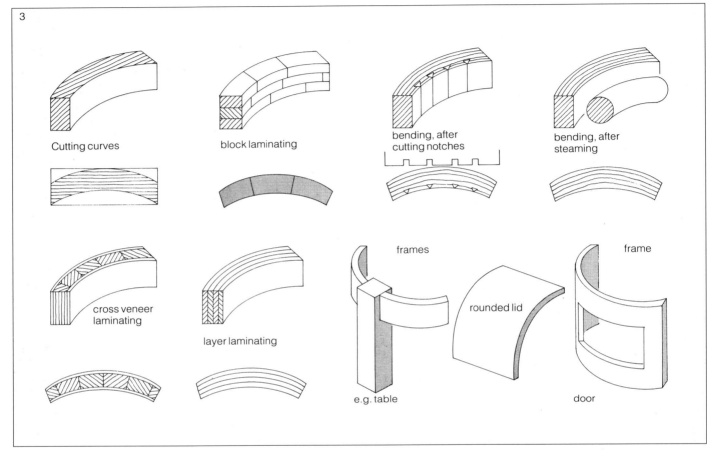

Cutting curves

block laminating

bending, after cutting notches

bending, after steaming

cross veneer laminating

layer laminating

frames

rounded lid

frame

e.g. table

door

Cutting shapes out of solid wood is simple, but has the disadvantage that the short grain in long curves might split when subjected to pressure.
Sawn wood may be bent by cutting small notches, or by the use of water and steam. Beechwood is particularly good for steam-bent chairs.

Blocked or veneered wood lamination, even when combined with one or more work-processes, is widely used, particularly in the production of chairs and other seating.
Shaped parts made of solid wood or manufactured board are more common than is generally assumed,

and can be found in round table frames or curved door frames.
In the past, developments in shaping wood were particularly popular during such eras as the Rococo. Now, the technical possibilities are endless. Almost anything can be turned, bent or curved.
The necessary materials, from wood and glue to plastic, are available everywhere and in every quality that could be desired. A particular choice is usually governed by the price, which almost always varies with the number of workpieces to be produced and therefore, as often as not, favours multiple production.
Unfortunately, creative criteria do not often receive their due consideration. However, it should not be forgotten that every contribution, no matter how small, helps to fashion our environment. We cannot be too aware of this responsibility.

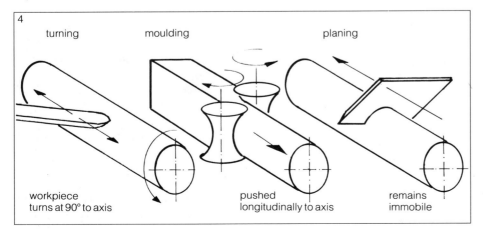

turning   moulding   planing

workpiece
turns at 90° to axis

pushed
longitudinally to axis

remains
immobile

Sawn wood can be made into a multitude of shapes by curving, bending or laminating. Compressed wood can also be formed into many shapes and achieves great rigidity, which is why its use has greatly increased. Chair-making and industry nowadays depend on the use of shaped parts. The technique of bending wood is today so refined that any shape at all in furniture or furnishings can be economically produced from manufactured board. Bent wood is composed of a number of layers of veneers of varying thicknesses, which are pressed together with great force, usually at high temperatures, during which process they are often densified.

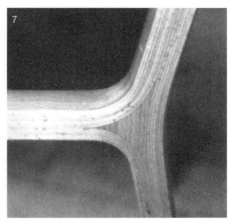

Fig 8 shows the effectiveness and possible uses of wood-strengthening. The methods can best be demonstrated by folding paper, bending tin or gluing boards.

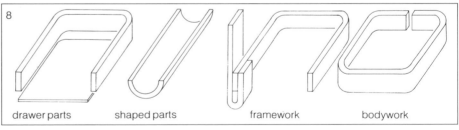

drawer parts   shaped parts   framework   bodywork

The strain put on bodywork and frames is particularly great where furniture is concerned. This aspect of design must be considered before embarking on any construction.
Furniture parts curved in various directions can be compared to the shapes used in car-body construction today. The desire to design inspired these constructions, which were then constantly improved.

Uses

Containers

Plates and bowls are turned in two working processes, while jars with lids, in principle at least, require four. The choice of wood plays an important rôle in the design of all containers. First the outer and then the inner sides are turned. The surface is often treated as soon as the individual parts are finished.

The shape of the rims of plates must be considered carefully, both to look at and to touch. During turning special care must be taken to avoid mis-shaping caused by the wood warping.

Bowls, both large and small, are specially shaped in all their details, inside and outside as well as at the rim, feet and base. It is popular to turn thin-walled bowls: but this requires repeated checking, which means that the work at the lathe has to be interrupted.

Jars are characterised by their lids, which also distinguish them from bowls. There are several different ways of fitting lids. Fitting the insides of jars with insets is an entertaining game which has artistic value. The photo shows a very beautiful piece of work made by the master turner, Professor Gottfried Böckelmann from Hildesheim, taken from the catalogue of the Focke Museum in Bremen.

Ring boxes have central openings in the form of either a hole or a hollow. There is something very attractive about these objects.

Beakers and goblets are often long-stemmed drinking vessels which are only occasionally made of wood nowadays.

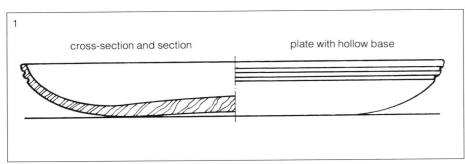

1

cross-section and section | plate with hollow base

Important aspects of plate design are the diameter, the depth, the choice of wood, the finished surface and the shape of the rim.

The rim may be wide or narrow, horizontal or sloping, smooth or profiled.

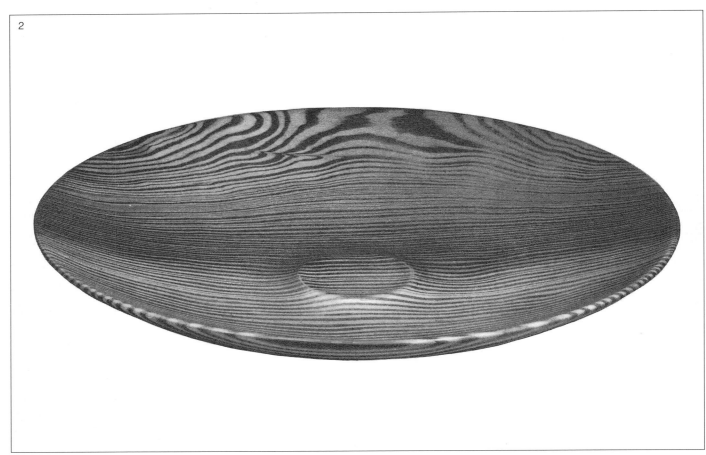

2

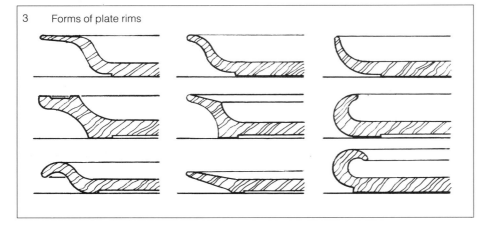

3 Forms of plate rims

The outer sides of plates slope down towards the centre. They may be more or less smoothly rounded, concave or curved. The inner sides are designed either parallel to or independently of them.

Some rare examples demonstrate undercutting.

The base may be raised or slightly hollowed for the plate to stand firmly.

Figs 7-9 show respectively: an ashtray made of compressed beech-wood, a cheese-dish varnished black, and a bread-board made of teak.

Fig 2 This plate of pitchpine measures 22 cm in diameter. In order to accentuate the grain the inside was turned only lightly, and was emphasised in the centre. The rim of the plate also sets an accent on the wood structure. (Designed and turned by Johann Winde.)

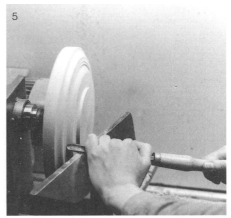

A plate is to be turned from a piece of cherry-wood (Figs 4-6). The diameter is 24 cm, the height 4 cm. The blank must be dry and absolutely free from cracks. When it has been marked out, it is bandsawn to a disc and mounted on a screw chuck.

The underside of the plate is given a rough profile with a gouge. A central elevation of 5 cm diameter is left so that the workpiece can later be mounted on a three-jaw scroll chuck.

The unwanted wood is roughed working from the edge of the disc outwards. The base is smoothed with a skew chisel. A parting tool is used to give it an exactly straight edge.
The rest of the process is shown on the following pages.

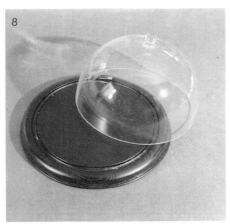

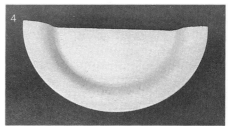

When the outside of the plate has been turned as shown on the previous page, it is sanded.

Work on the inside is not begun until the outside is finished.
The plate is mounted the other way round on a three-jaw scroll chuck.
A roughing gouge is used to turn the inner contour, working from the outside edge towards the centre.

When working with a large piece of wood, the possibility of warping must be considered (see Fig 9). Consequently the plate base should be turned on the outer side of the wood, where it may later become hollow. If the base of the plate is turned towards the inner side of the wood and then warps, the plate will wobble.

When the plates turned are too thin to be mounted on a screw chuck, one side must be planed so that it can be mounted securely between a faceplate and the tail centre.
Sandpaper is first stuck to the faceplate so that it has a better grip on the wood.

A small hardwood disc used as a jaw is set between the tail centre and the workpiece. The upper edge of the plate can then be worked (see Fig 10).

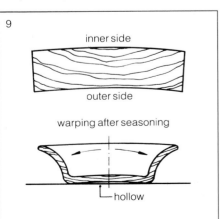

9
inner side

outer side

warping after seasoning

└─hollow

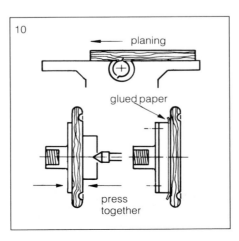

10
planing

glued paper

press
together

Using glued paper is another method for mounting a plate. A wooden disc is screwed to a faceplate and a layer of strong paper (not newspaper) is glued between it and the blank. The area of glued paper should be as large as possible. Pieces mounted this way must be turned carefully using little pressure, so that they do not become unstuck.
When the turning is completed the workpiece is removed from the disc with a thin knife, and the remains of the paper and glue from its base with a scraper.

The bowls in Figs 13-21 were made by the following:
Johannes Kunz, Neuenburg (Fig 13)
Anke Kusber, Hanover (Fig 14)
Volkmar Köllner, Schlitz (Fig 19)
Günther Kössling (Fig 20)
Bruce Mitchell (Fig 21)
The photographs are taken from the catalogue of the Focke Museum in Bremen.

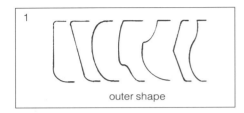

1 outer shape

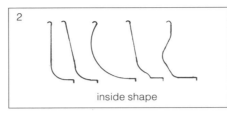

2 inside shape

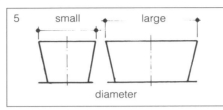

3 base shape, inside

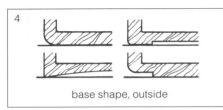

4 base shape, outside

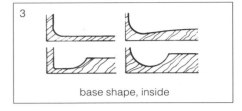

5 small large diameter

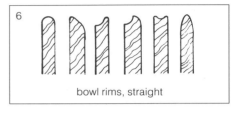

6 bowl rims, straight

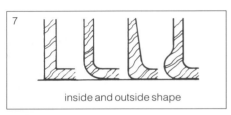

7 inside and outside shape

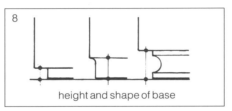

8 height and shape of base

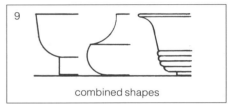

9 combined shapes

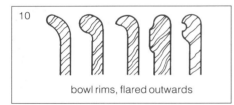

10 bowl rims, flared outwards

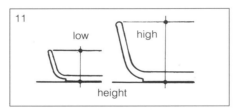

11 low high height

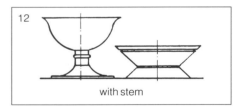

12 with stem

13

14

Figs 15 and 17: Two large bowls, each with a diameter of about 35 cm; above made of teak, below made of zebrawood (both designed by Johannes Kunz, Neuenburg).

The simple, straightforward shape sets off the lively, almost marble-like grain to advantage. Ornamental decoration can enliven the shape of objects made of wood with a very subdued grain.

The only differences between the production of a large bowl and a small one are in the diameter and the height.

The demonstration model shows a large bowl made of alder, a good turning wood which is easy to work. As with all workpieces with a large diameter, care must be taken to use wood with no cracks.

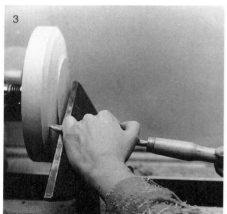

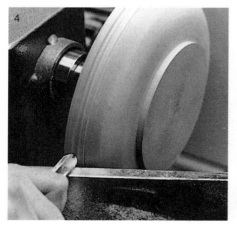

The side of the bowl is decorated with two grooves. The grooves are only as deep as the nose of the gouge, so the gouge may only be applied to the side of the bowl for a short time.

The outer side of the bowl should be given its final finish, i.e. waxed or oiled, before the inner side is turned.

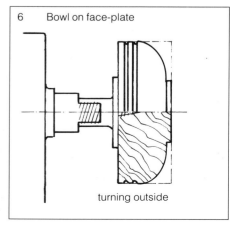

6   Bowl on face-plate

turning outside

The bowl is mounted on a three-jaw scroll chuck (Fig 7). The hole for the screw chuck can still be seen.
An indentation is made around the hole with a gouge and this is hollowed out until the hole can no longer be seen. The bowl is then turned from the edge towards the centre.

In Fig 8 the coarse marks left after roughing can be seen clearly. These must be smoothed away.
The inside base is turned smooth with a skew.
When the bowl has been sanded and sealed, the grain stands out well.

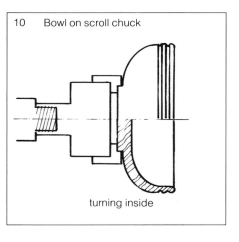

10 Bowl on scroll chuck

turning inside

12

The small bowl in Fig 1 was turned from a piece of well-seasoned oak. After the centre point was found, a circular arc was marked on the blank.

1

To fix the blank to the screw chuck a hole 8 mm in diameter was bored to a depth of about 1 cm into the wood, and the blank then cut to a polygon. The larger the diameter of a bowl, the more important it is to make the shape as cylindrical as possible before turning, so that the blank does not vibrate or hit the tool rest.

Figs 5 and 6 show a screw chuck and the mounting of a blank on it. The wood must be screwed as straight as possible on the thread for a flush fit against the faceplate.

The outside of the bowl is roughed down to a cylinder shape at a turning speed of about 800 rpm.
The faceplate turning of the body of the bowl is also done using a gouge, with the tool rest appropriately swung round towards the workpiece.

The outside slowly takes shape as the wood is cut off little by little, from the centre outwards. A raised base of about 70 mm diameter and 6 mm height is left on the bowl. This is important for attaching the bowl to the three-jaw scroll chuck. A parting tool is used to give the base a neat, angular cut.

Now the inside of the bowl can be turned. This is described on the following pages.

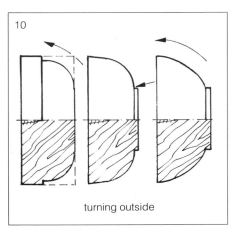

turning outside

The inside of the bowl is turned here, when the turning of the outside — described on the preceding pages — has been completed.

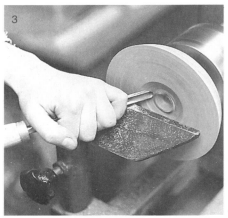

The bowl is mounted on the three-jaw scroll chuck (Fig 1) which means that the inside can now be hollowed out.

During hollowing out, the gouge is led from the edge towards the centre, the lathe speed being about 1200 rpm. The hole for the screw chuck can no longer be seen.

The thickness of the bowl wall is marked with a roughing gouge, about 1 cm wide. The bowl is gradually hollowed out from here to the centre until the correct inner shape emerges.

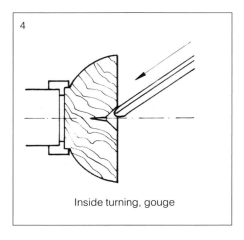

Inside turning, gouge

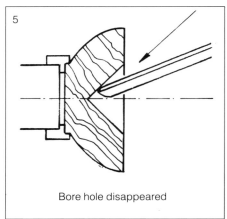

Bore hole disappeared

The wall thickness is tested with the fingers, so it is necessary to keep interrupting the turning process.

If the wall thickness increases considerably towards the base of the bowl, hollowing must continue. The outside and inside shapes should resemble each other.

While the rim is being formed, it should be tested again and again until it is pleasant and positive to touch.
Finally the base of the bowl is smoothed with a skew chisel. Blemishes should be removed carefully. Afterwards the final finish is given.

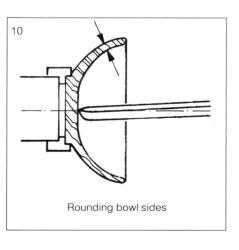

Rounding bowl sides

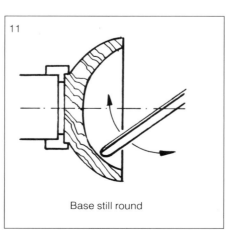

Base still round

The design of a jar is determined by several factors: technical, functional, and creative.

The proportions of the jar and its parts, i.e. the body and the lid, are just as important as the choice of material with regard to the type, structure and colour of the wood.

There are various possibilities for inside and outside shaping; the shapes may correspond to each other or be quite different. In the latter case, the element of surprise caused on opening the jar improves the overall effect. This does not always meet with approval, however.

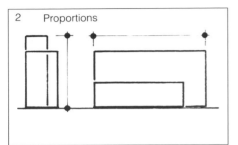

2 Proportions

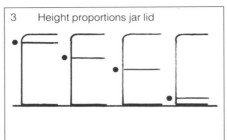

3 Height proportions jar lid

4 Inside shapes

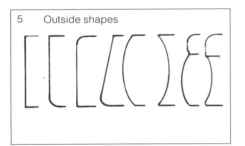

5 Outside shapes

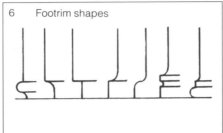

6 Footrim shapes

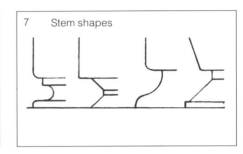

7 Stem shapes

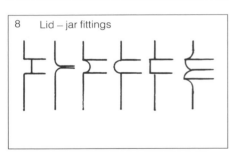

8 Lid – jar fittings

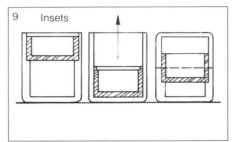

9 Insets

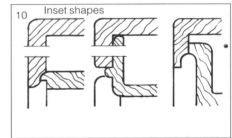

10 Inset shapes

Bases and footrims complete the bottom part of the jar; here it either sits firmly on a table or raises itself from it.

Inside jar-fittings in the form of walls are rare in turned work, and must be inserted afterwards.

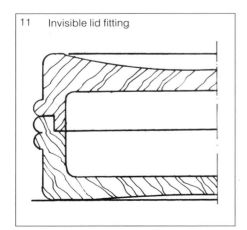

11 Invisible lid fitting

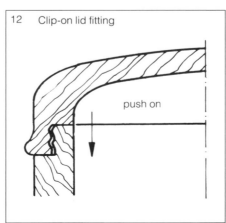

12 Clip-on lid fitting

push on

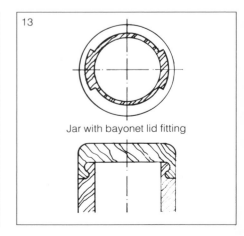

13

Jar with bayonet lid fitting

Jar lids have a special surface, rim and knob design. The knob or grip may extend above the top of the lid, or it may recede so as to be level with it. Small jars do not need such an aid to opening if the outside of the lids can be grasped with one hand.

Jar lids fit with simple or hidden joints; the actual fit may vary in tightness. Screw-on, clip-on or bayonet fittings are rarely found, as they are both complicated and expensive to make.

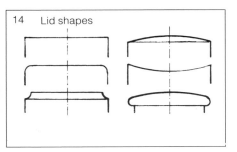

14   Lid shapes

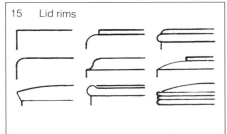

15   Lid rims

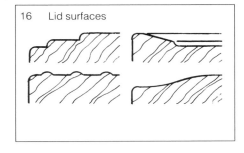

16   Lid surfaces

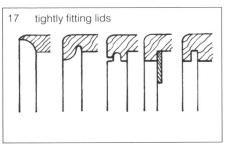

17   tightly fitting lids

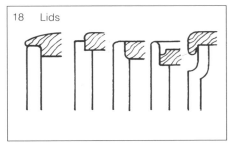

18   Lids

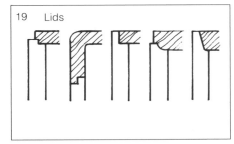

19   Lids

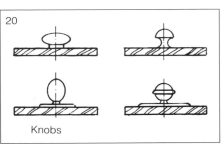

20

Knobs

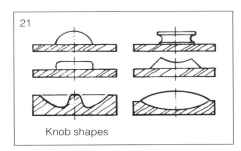

21

Knob shapes

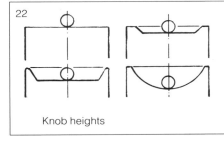

22

Knob heights

Insets in jars, also turned, can be attractive additions. The inner jars may be set at very different levels. Inserted at the top, they will show up immediately. At the base, however, they are very difficult to find, like secret compartments.

The place where an inset is fixed cannot be seen at all from outside the jar. Insets may also serve as a lid for the outer jar.

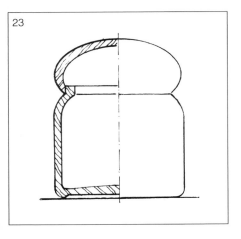

23

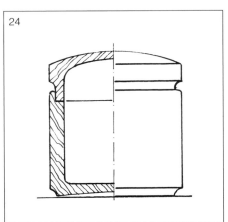

24

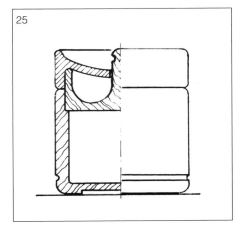

25

111

The turning of a lidded jar needs
careful planning. Individual steps
must be taken into consideration.
The lid of a small jar is first turned out
of a blank and later fitted on the other
way around (see Fig 2).

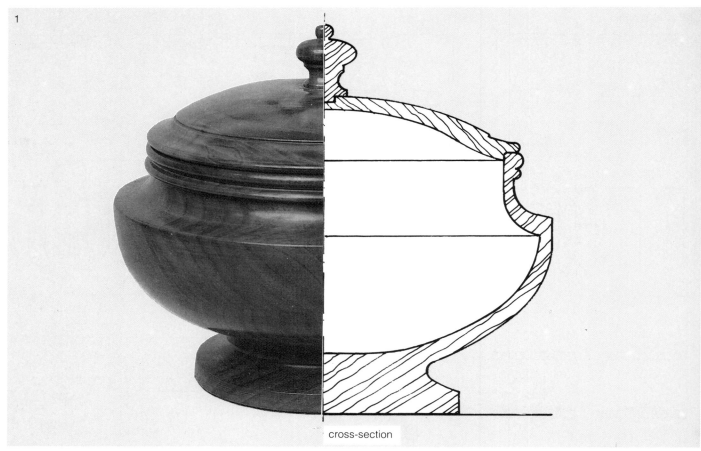

cross-section

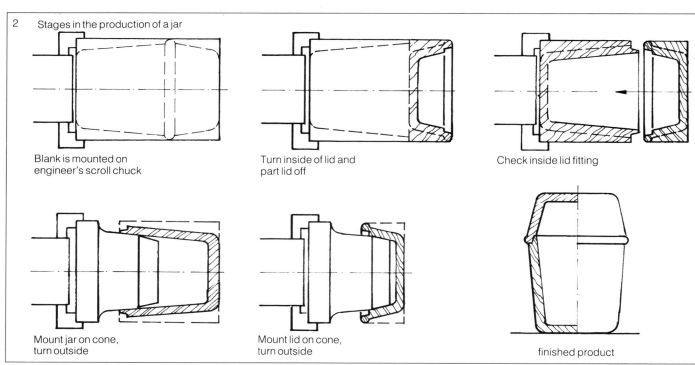

2 Stages in the production of a jar

Blank is mounted on
engineer's scroll chuck

Turn inside of lid and
part lid off

Check inside lid fitting

Mount jar on cone,
turn outside

Mount lid on cone,
turn outside

finished product

The contrast between two very similar jars (Figs 1 and 3) allows a comparison of the details and makes their different effects apparent. (These jars were designed and turned by E.N. Pearson.)

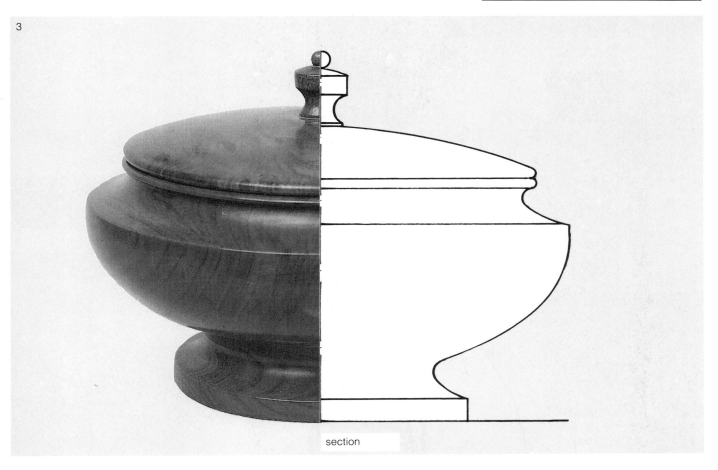

3

section

Wooden jars do not necessarily have to have wooden lids. The jar in Fig 4 has a metal lid, which may be extremely thin.
The jars on the following page illustrate the reverse use of different materials, i.e. wooden lids on glass bases.

4

5

6

1

2

3

4

The lidded jar (Fig 1) was made out of a walnut blank. This was divided into two parts and turned down into a cylinder. The taller part forms the base of the jar, the shorter part the lid.

Figs 5 and 6: wooden lids on glass jars.
Fig 7: antique wooden money box, turned and painted.
Similar jars, with cylindrical bases, are shown in Figs 10 and 11.

5

6

7

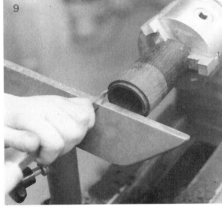

In Fig 4 the base of a jar is mounted on a screw chuck. At this stage its dimensions are two-thirds larger than the finished size.
(Fig 8) The base of the jar is now turned around and mounted on an engineer's scroll chuck.

The hole for the opening is shaped with a Forstner bit. The inside is then hollowed out with a gouge.
The thickness of the side is tested by hand. A rabbet is carefully turned with a parting tool to accommodate the lid (see Fig 9). The base is now complete.

The turning of the lid is demonstrated on the following pages.

The base of this jar was turned separately from the lid. Its production has been dealt with on previous pages – the turning of the lid is demonstrated here.

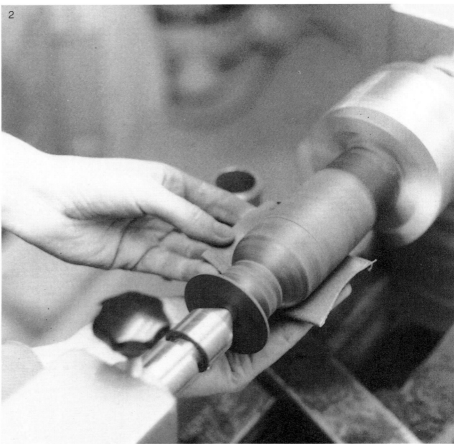

Fig 4: open jar of pitchpine (design: Günther Kunst, Zetel).
Fig 5: ceramic sugar jar with turned, teak lid and cork seal.
Fig 6: two small jars with high lids, one fitting externally, the other inside the jar.

First the lid is given its outside shape, apart from the very top which is turned later. A hollow and a 'negative' rabbet are then worked on the inner side.

The measurements of the lid rabbet must be compared with those of the base. The lid and base are put together and the fit tested. Slight inconsistencies in the joint can be corrected by sanding.

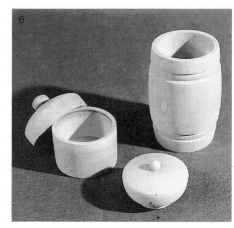

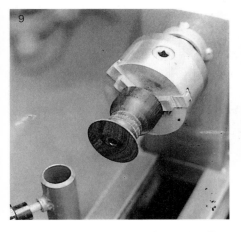

Fig 12: jar with bayonet-fitting lid. The lid is put on the jar and locked into position with a quarter turn.
Figs 13 and 14: jar with a distinctive base which matches the lid. Turned in untreated red beech and used as a vase for dried flowers.

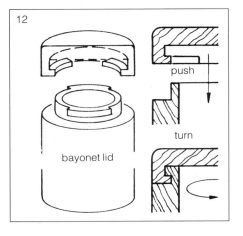

bayonet lid

push

turn

117

Ring boxes are strangely attractive, both in their design and in their use. The central hole or cavity invites the user to put something through it or into it. It is this inviting shape that makes ring boxes so special.

The base of a ring box with a hole is shown here in various stages of completion. The inside of the box has a high edge at the centre (see Figs 1, 2 and 3).

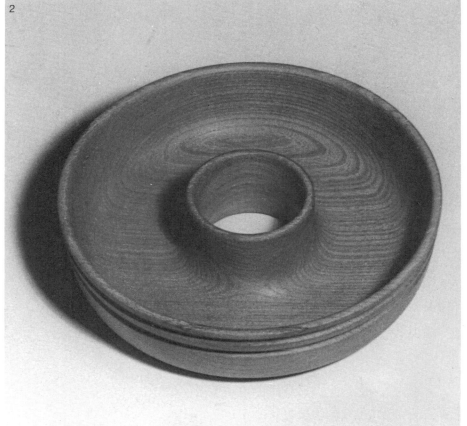

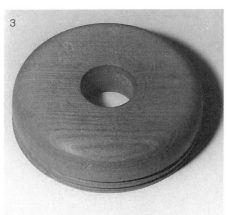

The diagrams show variations on this theme:
Fig 5: a ring box with different lids, and a knob or a hole in the centre.
Fig 6: a ring box with a high-arched, ring-shaped lid.
Fig 4: a ring box with a raised centre, terminating in a knob, around which the lid is placed.

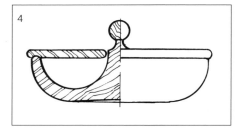

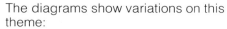

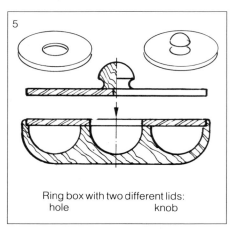

Ring box with two different lids:
hole   knob

Ring box with arched lid

Ring box with central hole

ring box   Isometric drawing

Fig 8: Ring box with a closed central cavity and an arched lid with an accentuated rim contour.

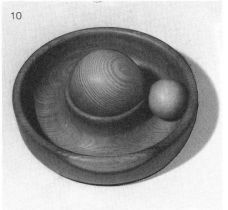

The ring box in Fig 12 has two lids. The central compartment is designed for keeping rings in and the outer cavity for necklaces. The double lid is a particularly attractive feature. It arouses curiosity and ensures that part of the jewellery is not discovered until the second phase of opening.

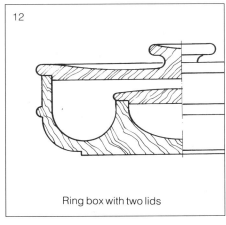

Ring box with two lids

Goblets can be turned from one piece or from several individual pieces of wood. The second method saves material, as it allows odd pieces to be used up. Bowl, foot and stem are glued together after being turned.

Hollowing out is begun using a Forstner bit and completed with a gouge.

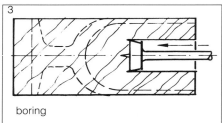

1 Goblet – in 3 parts

bowl

stem

foot

2

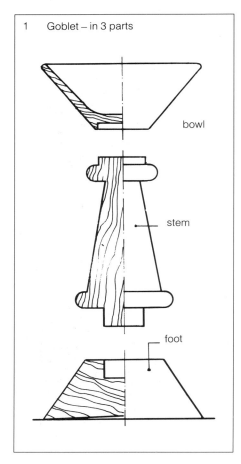

3

boring

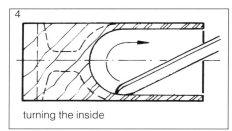

4

turning the inside

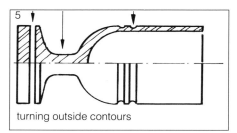

5

turning outside contours

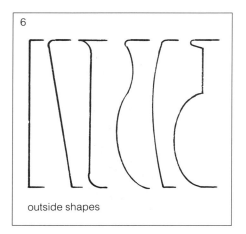

6

outside shapes

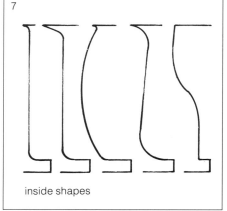

7

inside shapes

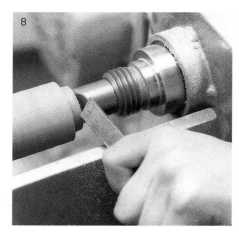

8

Beakers often have a long stem; goblets always do. They have now become rare, as they are not very easy to drink out of.

As far as design is concerned, however, turning goblets or beakers is still a rewarding job.

Goblets are usually only in demand for decorative purposes. Beakers, on the other hand, are everyday objects with a variety of functions.

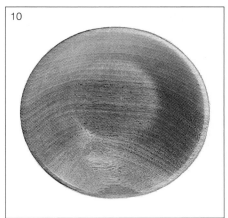

The proportions and dimensions of the individual parts contribute just as much to the overall impression as the choice of wood and working of the details.

The beaker must be large enough to be of the required capacity and its rim must be kept thin to enable the lips to touch it easily.

The stem must be able to be grasped well, whether it is thick or thin, high or low, straight or bulbous at the centre. The foot ensures that the goblet will stand firmly, without appearing clumsy.

Depending on their size and shape, beakers may be turned in one or more pieces.

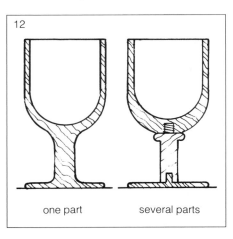

one part   several parts

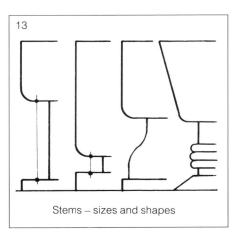

Stems – sizes and shapes

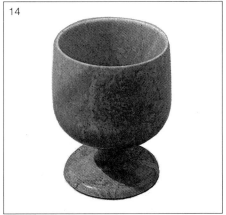

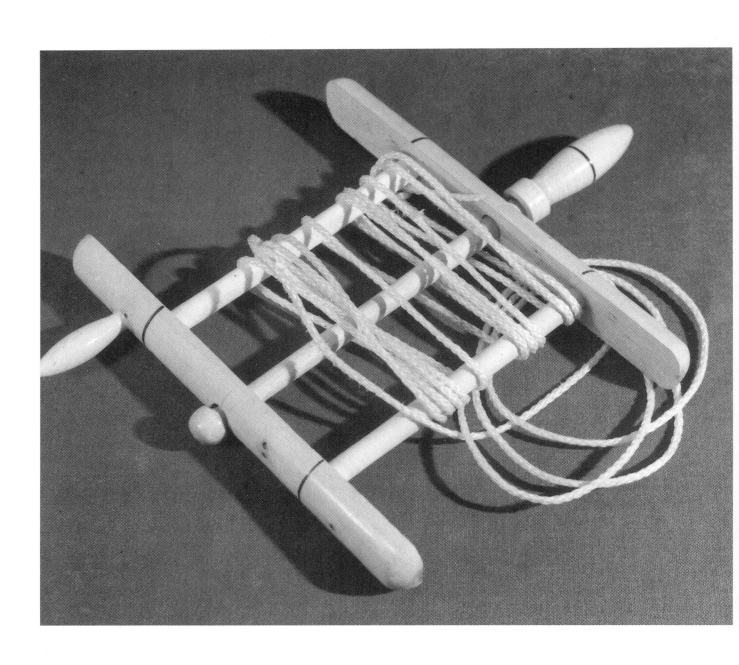

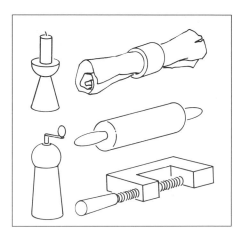

Making turned egg cups is good practice for the beginner. Variations are found mainly on the foot, stem and cup.

Pepper mills are often decorated and exaggeratedly large, which makes them part of the table decoration.

Serviette rings are very popular. The size, thickness of the sides and the decoration can be varied individually, making a serviette ring a very personal present.

Trays can be made large enough for a whole place-setting or very small, as coasters. Careful gluing is necessary on large pieces, to ensure that the surface stays level.

Kitchen equipment that can be turned includes rolling-pins, the handles of cutlery and other utensils. Tools often have parts made out of turned wood. It is just as usual to find turned darning mushrooms and washing-line winders as wooden taps and umbrella handles.

Spinning-wheels and swifts, whether antique or modern, are part of the established domain of wood-turning work. Stands, shafts and knobs on the framework and the spokes of the wheels have always been given richly decorated, detailed contours. New designs have difficulty in maintaining the quality possessed by the old spinning-wheels. One reason for setting the task of designing spinning-wheels is that spinning, like wood-turning, is becoming increasingly popular as a pastime.

Turning egg cups is a fairly easy way for the beginner to start producing everyday objects.

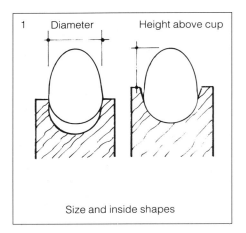

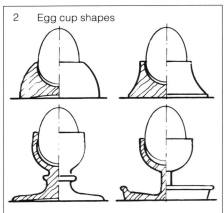

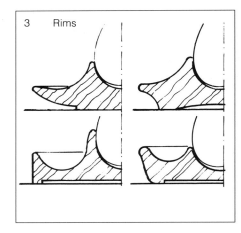

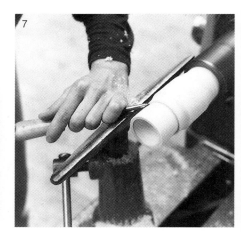

The base of the egg cup must be worked very carefully: the gouge is held so closely to the centre of rotation that it may easily bounce out and cut marks into the workpiece. These can be removed by sanding.

The cylinder-shaped blank is hammered firmly into a cup chuck. First the inside is hollowed out with a gouge. An egg can be used to check for size.

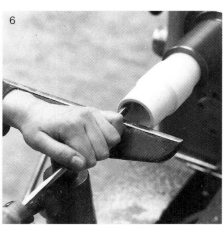

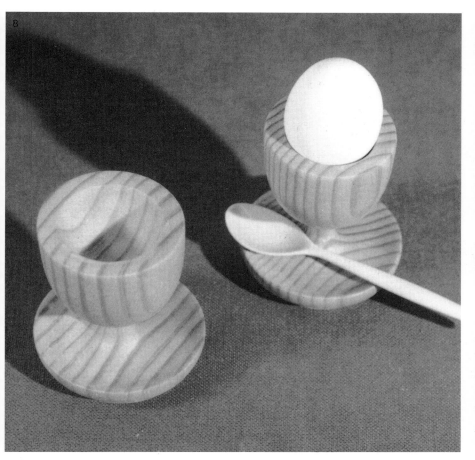

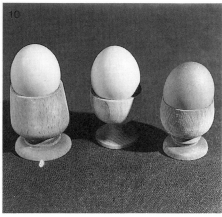

The outside is also cut with a gouge. In the example shown here (figs 11 and 12) the egg cup is given a hollowed stem and a foot. The final traces of turning are sanded away.

The egg cup is parted off with a skew chisel. The underside of the foot is not cut level, but hollowed slightly towards the centre to ensure that the egg cup stands firmly.

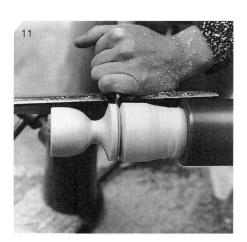

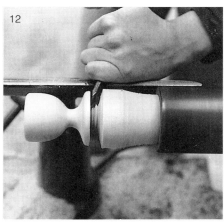

Pepper mills are constructed in a similar way to slender jars with lids. Instead of a lid, they have a knob that is connected to the axle of a grinding mechanism.

The inside of the shaft is bored hollow with a Forstner bit and fitted with the grinding mechanism at its base. The knob can be unscrewed and removed to refill the mill with peppercorns.

Medium-sized pepper mills are about 14-20 cm high, with an inside diameter of about 3 cm. The design of pepper mills can be varied greatly within the limits set by the function and the basic shape.

A pepper-grinding mechanism, complete with fitting instructions, can be bought from a good handicraft supplier. The grinding parts should be made of metal, not synthetic material.

1

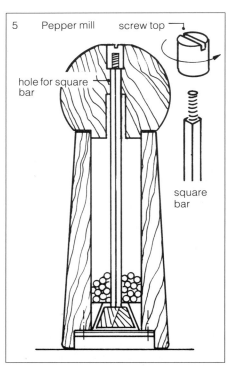
2

3

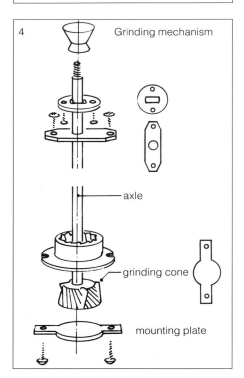
4   Grinding mechanism

axle

grinding cone

mounting plate

5   Pepper mill   screw top

hole for square bar

square bar

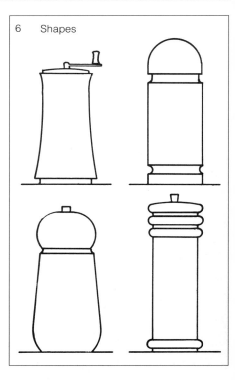
6   Shapes

Turning rings is an easier process than it appears at first sight. A deep bore-hole is made in a wooden cylinder with a Forstner bit. The required inner diameter can be achieved by cutting with a gouge. When the width of the ring has been marked, the surface is contoured, after which the ring is parted off. In this way several rings can be turned out of one blank in a short time.

For the surface treatment which follows, it is advisable to use a home-made spigot chuck made of soft-wood, on which the ring may be fixed from either end (see Fig 12).

Fig 13 illustrates different shapes in cross-section.

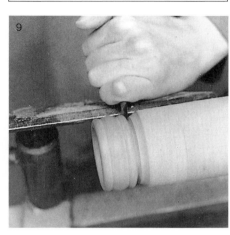

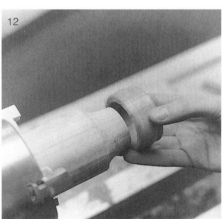

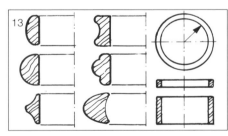

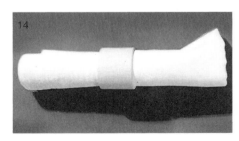

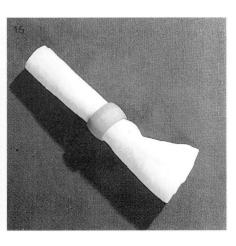

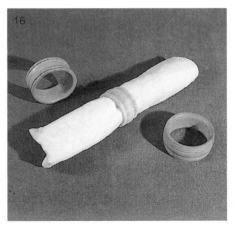

Turning wooden utensils for the table is very popular. The material is extremely attractive, both to the eye and the hand. The type of wood and its colour can be chosen to harmonise with the table-cloth, serviettes, cutlery, crockery and glasses.

Trays can be turned in many sizes, ranging from large trays suitable for a whole place-setting to small coasters. Fig 2 shows a tray with a raised rim, made of teak. It revolves on a ball-bearing.

Figs 1 and 3 show the top and bottom of a quiver-shaped container with a handle. The cylinder shape has been turned slightly conically on the inside and profiled on the outside. The handle was formed by cutting away the wood at the shaft.
The base, a plywood disc, was turned to fit by being pressed into a groove. This is why the inside is sloped.

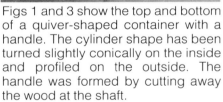

Kitchen equipment is usually made of turned wood for technical reasons, when it needs to be gripped all around and rotating or rolling movements are to be made. The range of utensils extends from pastry cutters and whisks to rolling pins.

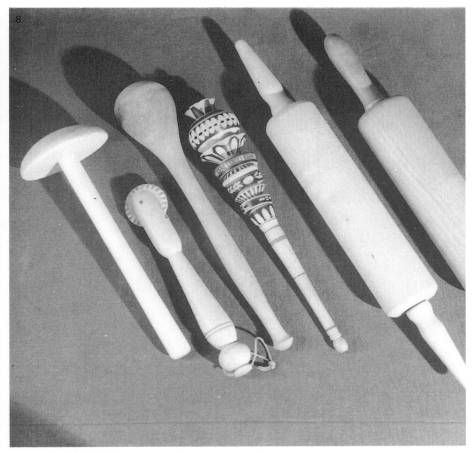

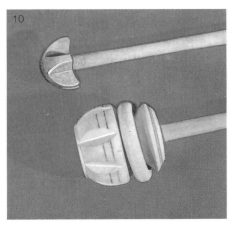

The old-fashioned whisks in Figs 9 and 10 have loose rings. These are both technically interesting to make, and functional and attractive in design.

Turned handles are found on cutlery, as well as, on, for example, two-handled chopping knives and corkscrews (Figs·11, 12 and 14).

All sorts of tools have parts made of turned wood. Handles of fretsaws, files, drills and rollers are shown in Figs 2, 9 and 11.

The whetstone case (Fig 1) is a fine example of how tools have survived and developed over the centuries. The proportions, such as the transition from the polygon to the rounded piece, are classic.

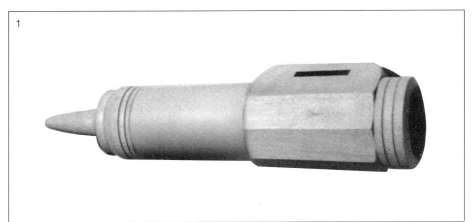

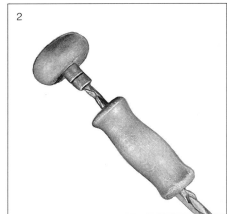

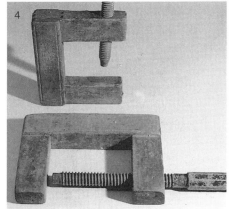

Darning mushrooms (Figs 3 and 6) have either a firmly glued stem or one with a thread which can be unscrewed.
The French knitting dolly (Fig 7) is contoured on the outside and has a hole bored right through the inside.

The ends of the knitting needles (Fig 8) are either turned as part of the needle or turned separately and fitted on afterwards.

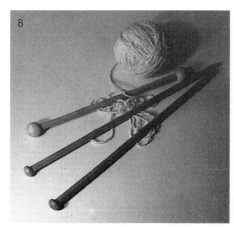

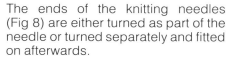

The handle of the old tailor's measure (Fig 10) consists of pieces of different coloured fancy wood glued together. It is decorated with a turned ivory ring. Fig 13: The umbrella handle has been turned conically in a wave-like pattern.

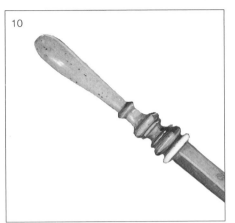

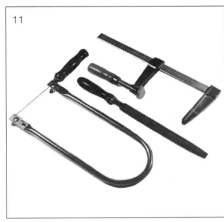

Fig 14: Wine rack made of dowelling of different thicknesses, fitted together and glued.

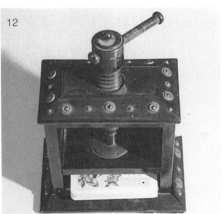

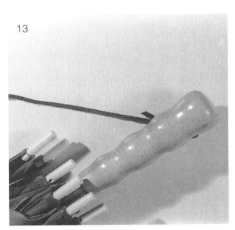

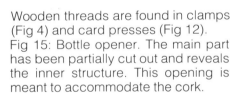

Wooden threads are found in clamps (Fig 4) and card presses (Fig 12). Fig 15: Bottle opener. The main part has been partially cut out and reveals the inner structure. This opening is meant to accommodate the cork.

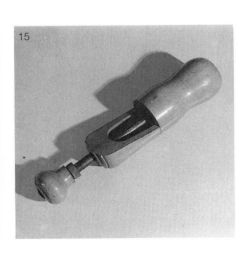

131

Antique spinning-wheels and swifts provide excellent evidence of how old tools were developed to perfection not only technically, but also in design. The craftsman's pride played just as important a rôle as the loving attention paid by the customer and the user. This is also shown by the inscriptions and insignia on these instruments, which were found not only in farmhouses, but also in the parlours of middle-class households.

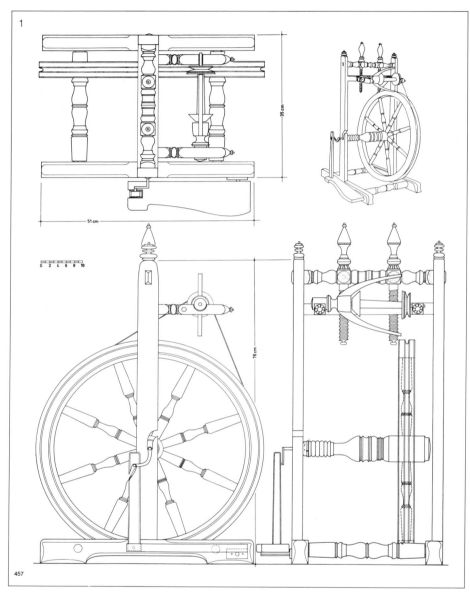

457

This is not the place to explain the technique of spinning-wheels in detail, but let this much be said: the large fly-wheels are mounted either below or beside the spindle, depending on the type. Occasionally, spinning-wheels are equipped with two spindles.

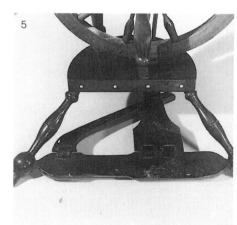

As the instruments are so fragile, hardwood was used, usually valuable fruit-tree wood and tropical wood, alongside large-pored oak and cheap beech.

Decorations made of ivory or bone can often be found on valued models. All the parts except for the actual wheel were given rich profiles and turned very finely.

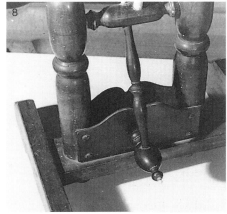

The hackles, used to prepare flax for spinning, were always more robust, first because the flax was pulled roughly and second because this was not done in the living quarters, but in the barn or out of doors. Nevertheless, this instrument was also designed with much affection.

Spinning-wheels are being built again today as increased leisure time allows people to spend more time on handicrafts.

Making slavish copies of old spinning-wheels is not very creative and quickly leads to mere imitation. The modernisation of old models often gets bogged down by ornamentation, which reduces the element of creativity.

Spinning-wheels which have the completely new form of a disc instead of a wheel appear disconcerting and helpless if compared to the matured antique models.

The spinning-wheel shown in Figs 1 and 2 has a wide frame that is new and original. It was affectionately painted by hand. (Design: Susanne Pracht.) The abstract quality of the decoration gives the wheel a certain freshness.

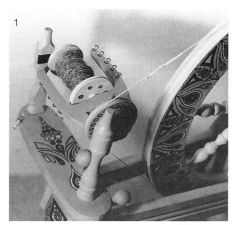

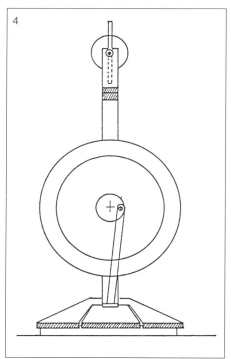

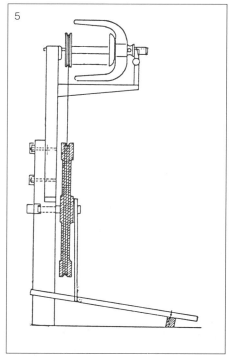

The spinning-wheel in Fig 6 is not as successful; although the frame is wide, the wheel is too small for it. The wave-like spokes of the wheel appear lifeless.

The spokes in Fig 2, however, have an antique profile which contrasts to the modern frame.

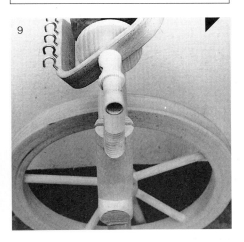

The spinning-wheel in Fig 8 is convincingly modern with its economic, consistently simple use of cylindrical forms. However, the uneven number of spokes and the large spaces between them have a negative effect on the piece as a whole.

The swift in Figs 12 and 13 is distinguished by its delicate, web-like appearance. The head and the clamp attachment are made of turned wood, as is the rod support.

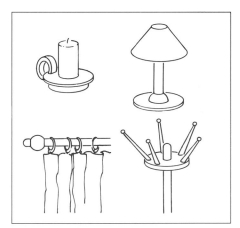

Candle holders are popular subjects for turning. They are variable in construction. Made of one or more parts, they may be portable or firmly installed.

Lamps usually stand on floors or tables. The feet, bases and stands are often laminated, either to accommodate electric wiring or for reasons of design. The bulb holders on wall and ceiling lamps are fixed in brackets, rings or crossed pieces of wood.

Frames for pictures and mirrors, and also for clocks and other objects, can be made from wood in a variety of sizes. Gluing before turning is done using tongue, tongue and groove or comb joints. The contours of the frames may be either smooth or very distinct, according to function and taste.

Hooks and rods have always been used to hang up objects, textiles in particular. Genuine hooks cannot be produced by turning; they are more like extended knobs. Rods are mounted either in fixed or movable (hinged) positions.

Hall stands have fixed central columns. Their bases and hooks are often sloping. All the parts can be turned with rich profiles, as they are easily mounted.

Curtain rods and rings made of wood are heavier than modern synthetic rails and hooks, but they have always been able to prove their value and they match rustic-styled interiors particularly well.

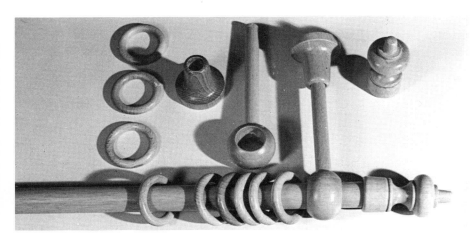

Candle-light has a warm, life-giving effect on the human eye and dispostion. From time immemorial the flame has been a positive symbol of power.
Because of this emotional value, the production of candle holders is a fascinating task for the turner.

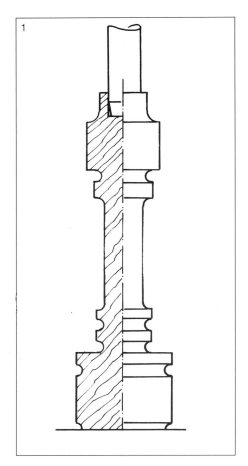

1

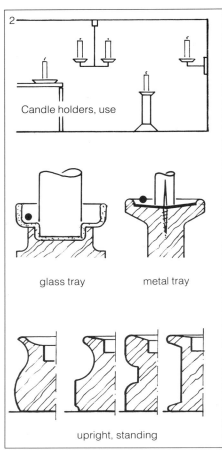

2

Candle holders, use

glass tray

metal tray

upright, standing

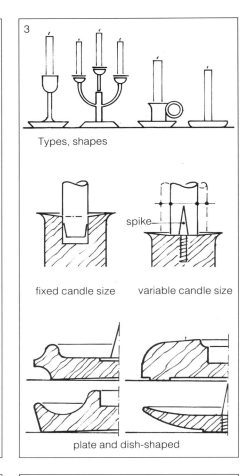

3

Types, shapes

spike

fixed candle size

variable candle size

plate and dish-shaped

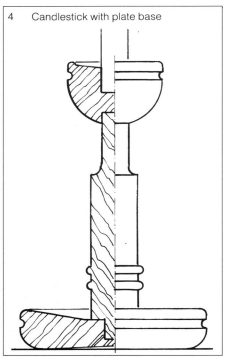

4   Candlestick with plate base

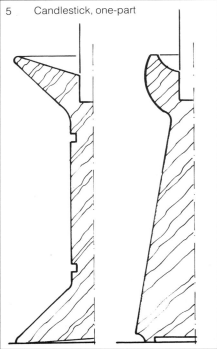

5   Candlestick, one-part

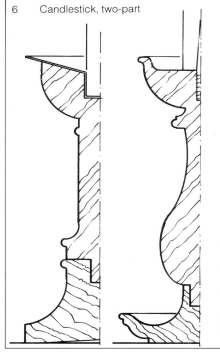

6   Candlestick, two-part

A candlestick is to be turned from a piece of pine (Figs 7-12).
A small pilot hole for the point of the centre is made in the end grain with an awl. Then the blank is mounted and the tool rest put into position.

The blank is first turned down to a cylinder with a roughing gouge. Then the contours to be made are marked on the cylinder and cut in with the point of a skew chisel.
A hollow is formed in the base with a roughing gouge. Further working processes are shown on the following pages.

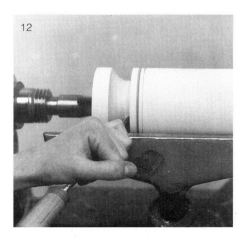

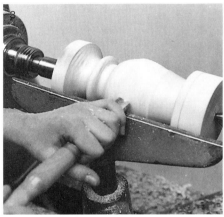

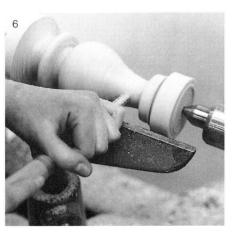

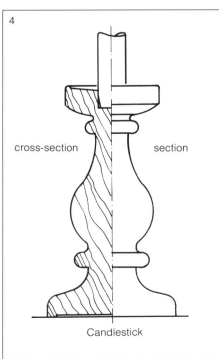

The preparation for this candlestick is shown on the previous page.

Now the shaft of the candlestick must be turned. The central part is given a bulbous ogee shape, which is turned with a gouge. The top of the candlestick must match the shaft.

cross-section   section

Candlestick

The various parts are worked over until the proportions fit together in harmony.
The surface is sanded with abrasive paper. Now the lively grain stands out clearly.

The top of the candlestick is given a bowl-like hollow to catch dripping wax. In order to do this, the tool rest is swivelled round at an angle (Fig 8). Care must be taken that the gouge does not touch the centre.

Finally a hole must be bored, wide enough for the candle to fit into. The elevation left where the tail centre was attached should first be chiselled off to give the Forstner bit a better grip.

The construction of a candle holder differs according to the number of candles to be held and where it is to be used – whether standing on a table or floor, hanging from a ceiling or fixed to a wall.

The candles are either pushed on spikes or into holes.
The wax drips down into small wooden, metal or glass trays.
Candle holders are carried by being grasped round the base or are held at the edge of the plate, sometimes by a turned handle.

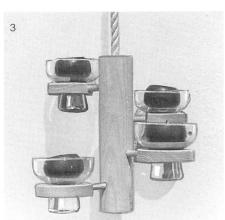

The candle holder in Figs 1-3, constructed of a few standard parts, is both very simple to produce and very variable. The actual candle holder and the drip tray consist of a glass held by a ring.
Fig 4: Wall candle holder with two wooden rings, dowelled to the semi-circular middle column.
Fig 5: Pinewood stand for a small candle.

Fig 2: A four-armed candle stand with a handle on the central column.
Fig 1 shows a variation of the theme with the candles arranged at different heights.
Fig 3 shows the same type of candle holder in hanging form.

Figs 7 and 8: A two-part cnadlestick for one candle, consisting of a long stem in a concave, circular base.

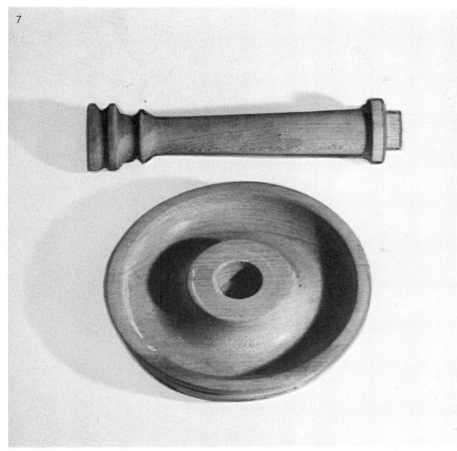

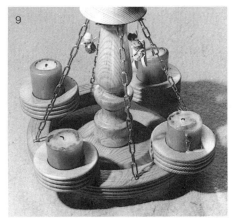

Variations in the shapes of the stems, the candle holders, drip trays and handles are shown in Figs 10-12.

Fig 9: Advent candle stand with four candles on a ring which is attached to a central column by chains. The candle holders and the ring have the same profiling. The top of the column conceals the points where the chains are attached.

Collapsible candelabra with many branches have been in existence for centuries. Their designs vary very much from one area to another.

The contrast between two versions coming from the same area in Northern Germany, but from different times, allows a comparison and evaluation of the details and their characteristic effect (see Figs 1-3).

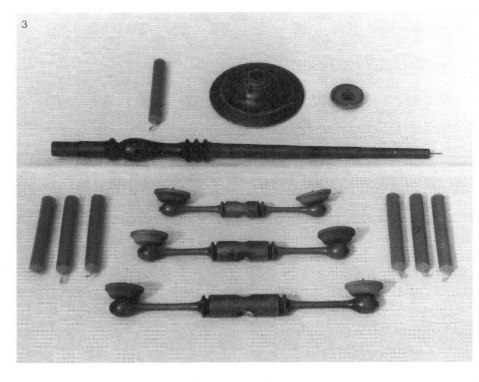

(left) Broder Burow, jar made of granadilla, laminated with castello, h. 95 mm, ⌀ 71 mm
(below) Broder Burow: bowl made of oak with rim of moor oak, h. 83 mm, ⌀ 240 mm

(right) jar of Indian palisander, h. 16 cm, ⌀ 10 cm

(left) Johann Kunst, bowl made of Swedish birch, h. 7 cm, ⌀ 15 cm

Imaginative table decorations can be made by combining various standard elements of a system.

Two candlesticks (Figs 6 and 8) with spikes to hold the candles clearly illustrate how different two objects with almost the same shape can be. This difference is due to the choice of wood, its structure and colour.

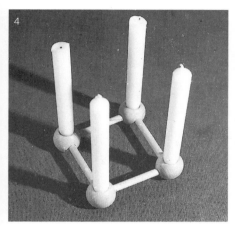

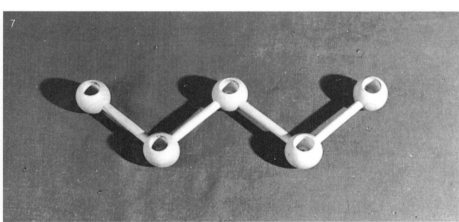

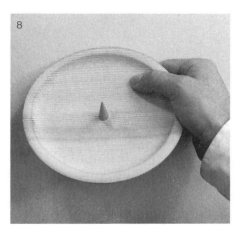

Fig 10: An Advent candle stand with a turned central column and a broad base. The ribbons which hold the wreath pass through holes bored in the top of the column.
Fig 9: Birthday-candle holders, made of flat pieces of wood turned to ring-shapes, are usually decorated by painting.

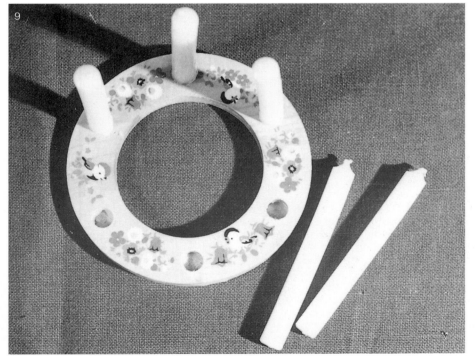

Even today it is still usual for lamps to have stands made of wood. As the stands are often found at eye or hand level, wood is a particularly suitable material to choose, especially for use in living areas, because of its well-known qualities.

The idea of turning lamp stands from wood suggests itself, since the light given by the lamp and its shade are already circular. Table, standard, wall or ceiling lamps can all have turned bases.

Fig 1 shows a painted, cylindrical, wooden lamp stand that has been turned to form a cone at the top.
The table lamps in Figs 3, 4 and 5 illustrate diversely-shaped shafts and bases.

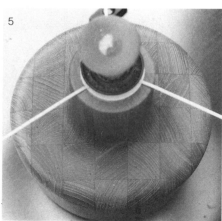

The standard lamps illustrated in Fig 10 and 11 show reverse accents in their technical details. The lamp in Fig 11 has an extremely large shade and a very flat base. The lamp in Fig 10 has a tiny bulb holder and an extremely large base. The effect of the lighting also contrasts – one lamp lighting downwards and the other up to the ceiling, which reflects the light indirectly.

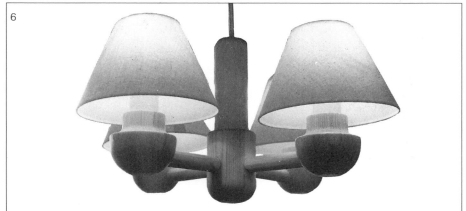

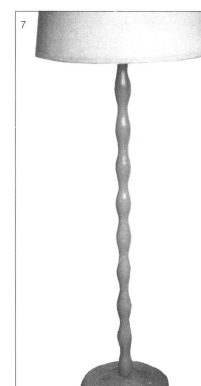

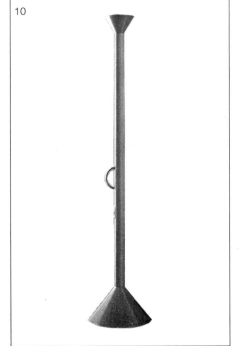

Lamps with a heavy base or wooden shaft are made of block-laminated wood, at least part of which is turned hollow. This means that less wood is needed, so that the stand is not so heavy and cannot split.

Block-laminating is also used when the wood is to be left as near to its natural state as possible, for reasons of design. Figs 4 and 5 on page 146 show a lamp stand made of blocked teak.

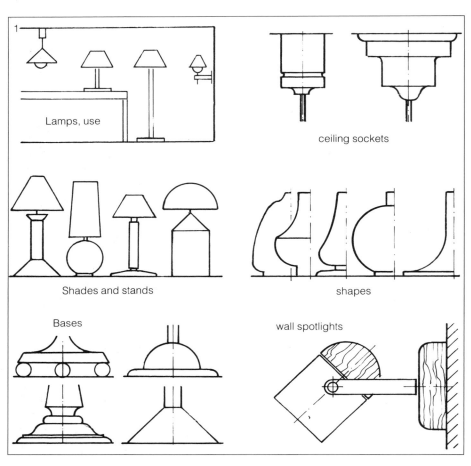

Lamps, use

Shades and stands

Bases

ceiling sockets

shapes

wall spotlights

The construction of hanging lamps can be extremely varied, and the number of lights may vary depending on whether the fitting is a normal lamp or candelabrum.
Bulb holders made of turned wood are often set on hoops, rings, crossed pieces or at the end of a fixed wooden arm.

The ceiling sockets must also accommodate the connectors and will fit better, as well as being easier to mount if they are made in two pieces. The socket covers are either screwed or locked into position (Fig 3).

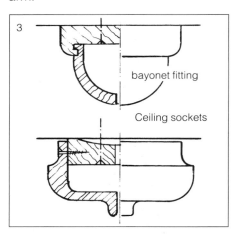

bayonet fitting

Ceiling sockets

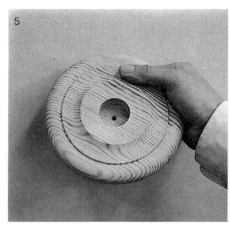

One particular feature of table and standard lamps is the base, which must stand firmly. To be really stable the shaft and the base must have an excellent fit, although this may be able to be dismantled, for reasons of production, assembly or transport.

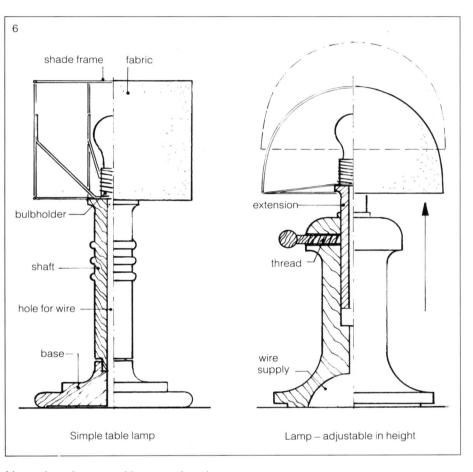

6

shade frame   fabric

bulbholder

shaft

hole for wire

base

Simple table lamp

extension

thread

wire
supply

Lamp – adjustable in height

7

Nowadays it goes without saying that the wiring of standard lamps is concealed along the full length of the shaft, which has either been laminated or bored hollow.
The problem of height adjustment can also be solved with shafts made of turned wood, as illustrated in Fig 6, right.

Wall lamps, in contrast to ceiling lamps, are attached to a wall in a fixed position, but they can also be adjustable.
Turned wall-socket covers with a profile are popular.

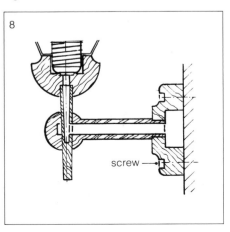

8

screw

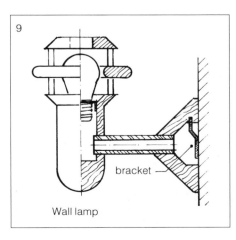

9

bracket

Wall lamp

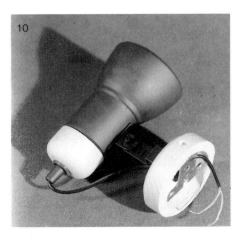

10

Frames form the technical and artistic borders of mirrors, clocks and many other kinds of instrument.

Round wooden frames need to be specially constructed before being turned. The run of the grain of the individual parts must not be so short that particularly slender frames would break.

Faceplates are usually used to turn frames. Thicker frames are screwed to the faceplate; thinner ones are glued.

The contours of a frame can be deep or shallow, smooth or profiled, sloping inwards or outwards, according to taste and purpose.

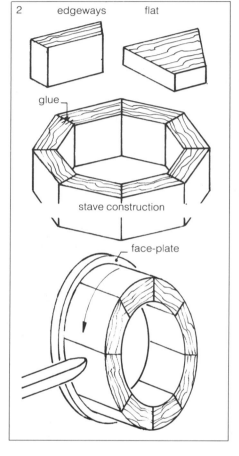

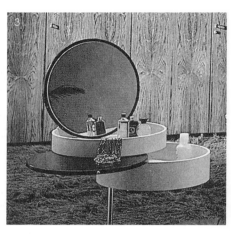

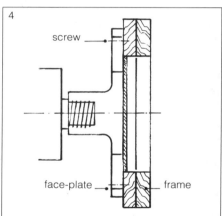

The parts of the frame must be very securely joined. Depending on the size and thickness of the frame, the pieces of wood can be joined with tongue and groove, tongue or even comb joints. Block-laminating results in a number of staggered, glued joints, and this must be taken into consideration if the surface is to be left in its natural state.

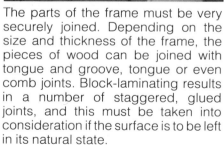

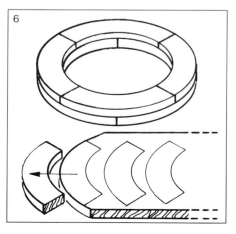

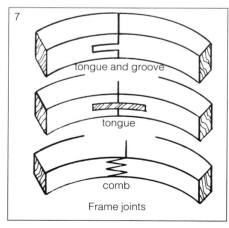

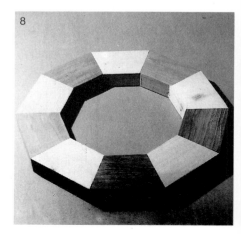

Frame joints

Whether or not the frame has a back, the picture, glass or instrument is always framed from the inside, so that its edges are concealed. Completely circular frames are turned in one piece; nowadays larger pieces may also be cut or moulded.

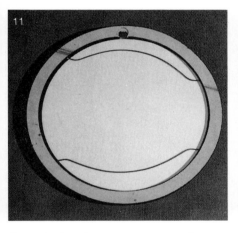

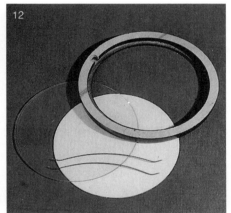

Rounded edges on square frames may also be made using turned discs or rings. These are divided into sections which are glued between the straight sides of the frame.

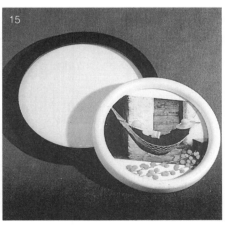

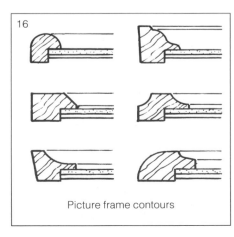

Picture frame contours

151

Hooks and rails have always been used to hang up, keep and dry all sorts of things, particularly textiles.

The row of hooks on a weaving loom (Fig 1) is made up of individually mounted pegs, turned from dowelling. The slightly flat knobs were easily turned because of the concial shape of the shafts.

Single hooks are generally fixed to walls by plate-like sockets (Fig 3). Series of hooks are mounted together on boards, or bored into posts (Figs 4 and 5).

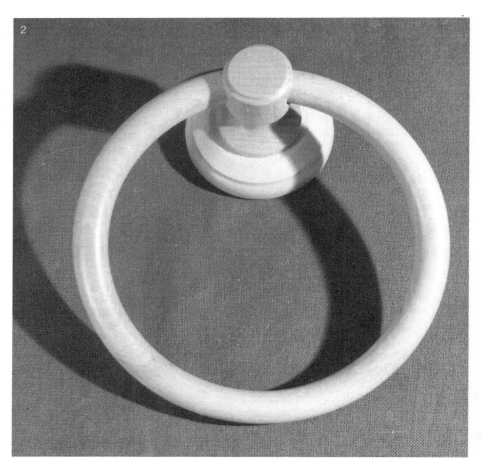

Wastage can be kept to a minimum by skilful design or production.
The wooden knob in Fig 3 was turned in different parts which were assembled later.

Turned coat hooks are not literally 'hooks', but rather 'extended knobs', yet they cannot be turned in any other way. They are usually thicker at the outer end to prevent the objects they hold from slipping off.

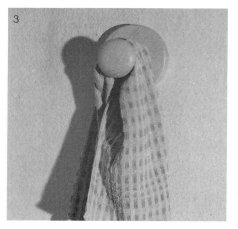

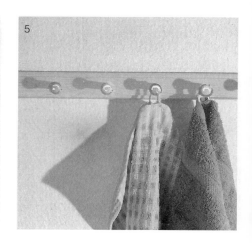

Loosely hanging rings like door-knockers (Figs 2 and 6) are often used for hanging towels. They are cut open so that they can be mounted in a knob, with the ends concealed. The run of the grain should be taken into account before the ring is cut, as the cut must be made into the side grain.

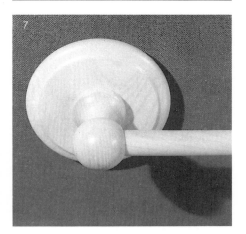

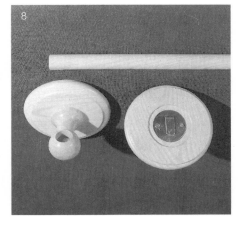

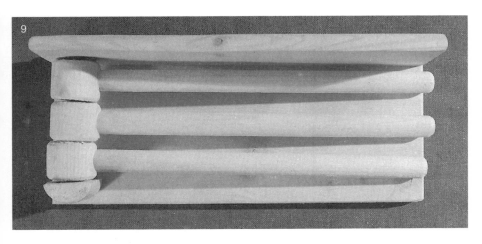

Rails enable towels to be hung up widthways. They can be fixed individually between holders (Fig 7) or combined with a row of hooks on a board (Fig 4). Hinged rails are very practical: on these several towels can be dried together and the rails then swung back to save space.

Rings which are mounted horizontally on walls (Fig 10) can be used for holding glasses or vases.

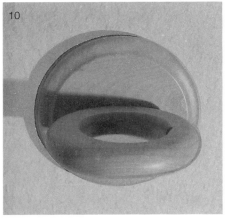

Turned hall stands usually have a strong central column, which is more or less richly profiled. The 'hooks' usually consists of rods or pegs bored at an angle and which have well-rounded ends.

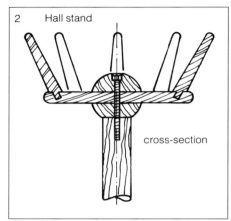

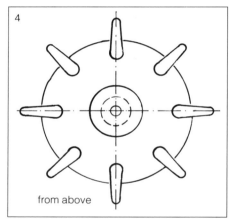
2 Hall stand

cross-section

4

from above

The antique towel rail in Fig 7 illustrates design in woodturning.

Knobs, often used for coat hooks (see Figs 3 and 5) are rarely found on coat stands (Fig 6).

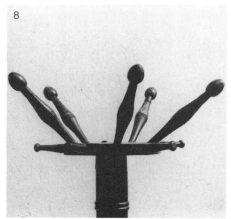

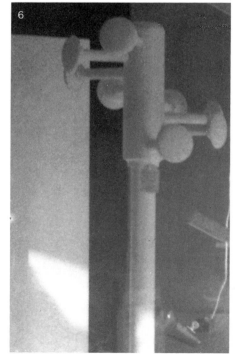

Curtain rods and rings made of wood have always been able to prove their worth alongside all sorts of other curtain rails. Particularly rustic versions are very popular in certain areas and for matching rustic-style furniture and fittings.

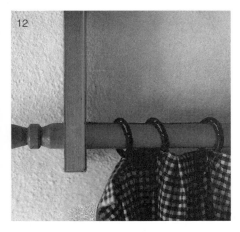

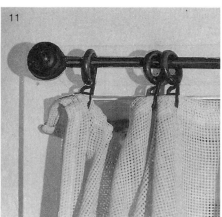

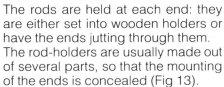

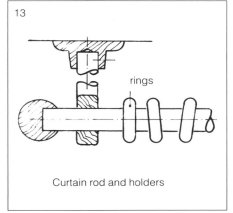

Curtain rod and holders

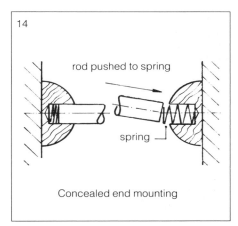

Concealed end mounting

The rods are held at each end: they are either set into wooden holders or have the ends jutting through them. The rod-holders are usually made out of several parts, so that the mounting of the ends is concealed (Fig 13).

Curtain rings, which look like enormous serviette rings, are used to hold draped curtains at the sides of windows (Fig 17).

Rods may be mounted using springs in both holders (Fig 14).
Where rods are mounted in plastic holders, this can be concealed by the use of wooden covers.
Wooden rosettes can be screwed to a wall and the rods mounted in them.

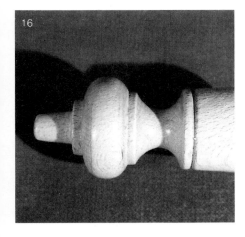

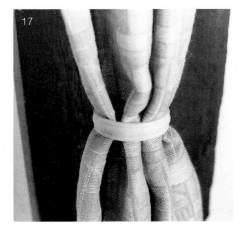

Toys

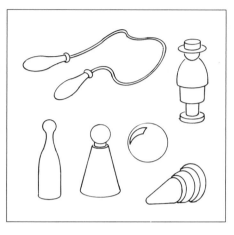

Children enjoy playing with wooden balls of all sizes, from marbles to bowls.

Turned wooden balls are also used to decorate furniture and fittings, such as chair-backs, bedposts or bannisters. Smooth or profiled wooden balls are either turned in the same piece as the post or mounted separately.

Beads, rings and discs are popular toys for small children. They can be strung together to make necklaces or even bead curtains.

Spinning tops which are worked with the fingers have an axle on which they twist. Tops worked by a whip have grooves for the string.

Counters are used by adults as well as children. One only has to think of ludo or chess.

Some counters or wooden dolls can be fitted inside each other; they can be turned either as individual figures or in series. Some wooden figures are available as semi-finished products, so even children can make their own nutcracker princes or jumping jacks.

Spires and cones made of wood provide interesting components for imaginative games.

One way of making toy animals is to turn a wooden ring or hoop and cut the animals out of this. This process is a special technique.

Skipping ropes, climbing frames and swings have many sorts of turned wooden handles, bars and beads.

Turning a wooden ball requires a sure eye as well as a great deal of practice and patience.

The cylindrical blank, in this case pinewood, is mounted between centres. When the central line has been marked, the wood to its left and right is removed, in the same process as turning a bead. The photographs clearly illustrate the work.

Finally, two stumps remain at the centres. These have to be removed. To do this the ball is firmly mounted sideways between a pair of home-made, press-fit chucks. Care must be taken to fit the chucks at the correct angle. (The work process is continued on the following page.)

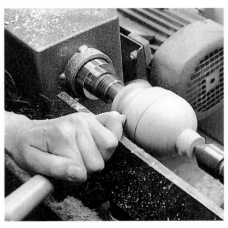

Wooden balls are used as toys, but are also popular on furniture and fitments as well as on other small items, or simply as abstract shapes.

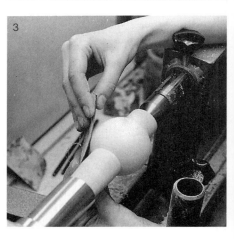

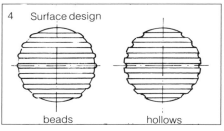

The pair of chucks must be made out of a softer type of wood than the workpiece, to prevent their denting the surface. The chuck on the revolving tailstock centre must fit snugly.

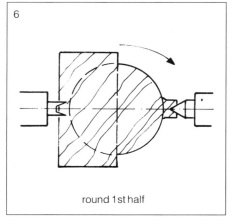

4   Surface design

beads   hollows

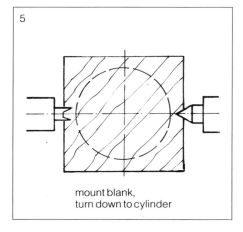

5

mount blank,
turn down to cylinder

6

round 1st half

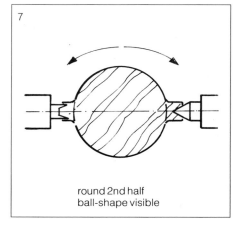

7

round 2nd half
ball-shape visible

158

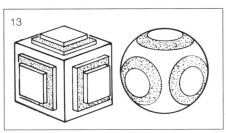

The roundness of the ball can be tested using a template or callipers. Interesting surfaces can be produced by gluing veneer-like blocks together. The example in Fig 16 is a masterpiece of precision.

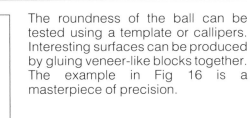

12 template   callipers

13

14 chuck rotates with workpiece

re-mount ball, turn stumps away, sand

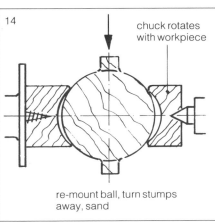

15

16

An enormous variety of bead shapes can be turned. Round beads and slender, bobbin-shaped beads are most common. Pear or bell-shaped beads, beads with pointed ends and profiled beads complete the assortment.

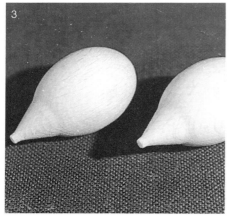

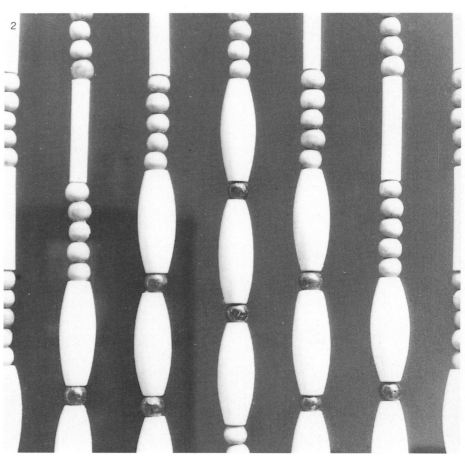

It is astounding how pieces of the same wood can look so different when they are not worked in the same way. The grain, in particular, appears completely different (see Fig 4).

The combination of different sizes, lengths, colours and numbers of beads is unlimited. Entire curtains of beads can be strung together.
Wood provides a wide scope to anyone with enough imagination.

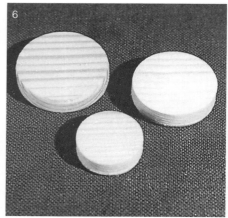

Heinrich Böckenhauer, turned objects

(left) Jack Mankiewicz, fountain pen made of amarant and Brazil wood

(right) fountain pen made of snakewood and granadilla

Wooden toys are well-known and time-tested, especially those for small children. By playing with turned wooden beads, rings and balls (as well as with building blocks, of course) children get to know the pleasant touch of wood, its surface and its various shapes from an early age. Classic wooden toys have lost none of their attraction.

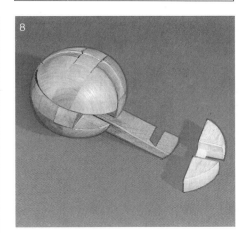

As is shown by the caterpillar (Fig 7) — made of parts of different coloured, varnished wooden balls and held together with a spring — it is possible even today to create new, up-to-date toys from wood.

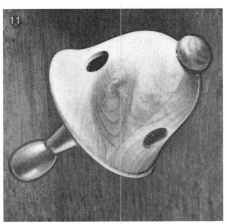

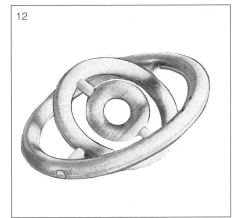

Yo-yos and tops are very easy to turn. To make a yo-yo, a simple piece of board is all that is needed. It should be as heavy as possible, however, to ensure that the finished article works properly.

The disc is mounted on a screw chuck and the deep notch for the string is cut with a parting tool. The hole left by the screw chuck can be bored open and then stopped up with a piece of dowelling.

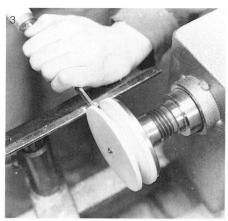

A loop is made in the yo-yo string, and then pulled tightly round the centre. Flexible string (e.g. fishing line) is best.

Fig 5: Ring elements made by Peer Clahsen from Schopfheim: exact fit and profiling fascinate children and adults.

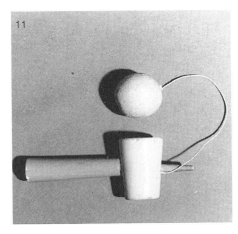

A spinning top should be made of heavy wood, e.g. oak or beech, so that it has enough momentum when spun. The roundness and the angle of the point, as well as the height and the type of wood used, are important. The flatter the angle of the point and the wider the upper part of the spinning top, the more smoothly it will spin.

A central axle made of a small rod will stabilize the top (Fig 10). It can be set in motion by twirling the rod between the fingers.

Figs 6-8 illustrate the turning of a simple top.

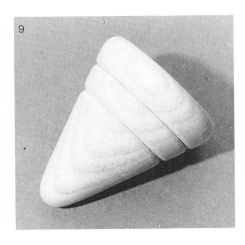

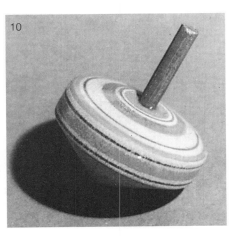

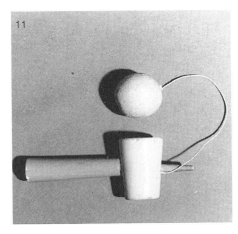

Turning chessmen is an interesting task for the amateur turner as well as for the professional. As the figures are relatively small (pawns 4 cm, king 7 cm), leftover pieces of wood can be used.

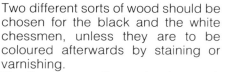

Two different sorts of wood should be chosen for the black and the white chessmen, unless they are to be coloured afterwards by staining or varnishing.

The figures are all cup chuck turned, without exception. In this way several figures can be turned, one after another, from one blank which is mounted in a cupchuck. When completed, they are cut off with a tenon saw.

It is advisable to use a template so that all the figures, especially the pawns, have the same measurements and proportions. Only the knight and the king's cross need to be carved.

Fig 10 compares the relative sizes of chessmen, using classic measurements.

The squares of the chessboard should be made of the same wood (veneer) as the chessmen for the game to be completely harmonious.

Round pieces of felt may be stuck beneath the bases of the figures.

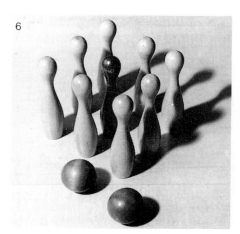

Fig 9: 'Russian' dolls turned hollow inside. Up to eight dolls can be put inside one another. The poplar wood used here is very richly painted.

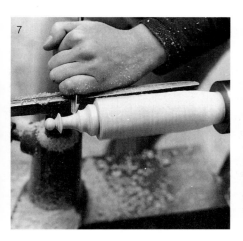

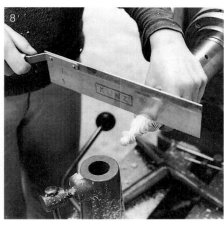

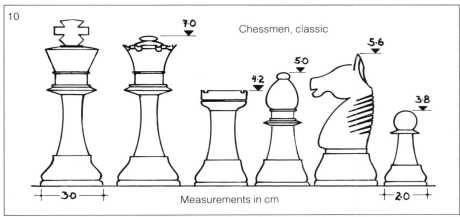

Chessmen, classic

7·0

5·6

5·0

4·2

3·8

3·0

Measurements in cm

2·0

Jumping jacks (Fig 13) and nut-cracker princes (Fig 15) are made to a large extent of turned parts.

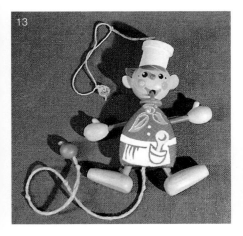

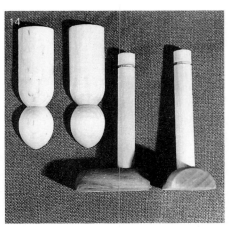

165

Ideas for different kinds of toys are shown on this page.

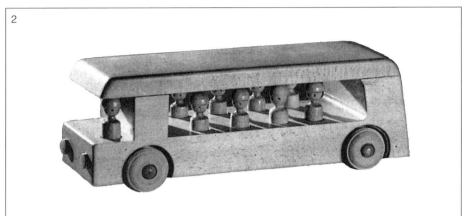

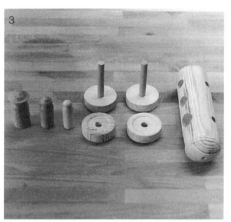

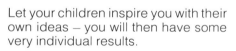

Let your children inspire you with their own ideas – you will then have some very individual results.

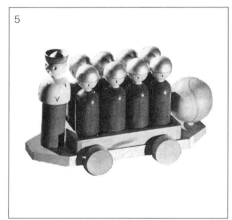

The realisation of ideas is a mutual experience for parent and child.

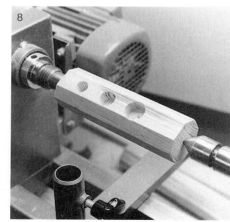

Cutting objects from turned rings is probably the most ingenious form of turning. It originated in the Erz Mountains in about 1800, but is practised to only a limited extent nowadays.

The rings are always turned from wood cut in the end grain. (All other turned objects are normally made of sawn timber cut from the side grain along the trunk.) Fig 10 illustrates the principle.

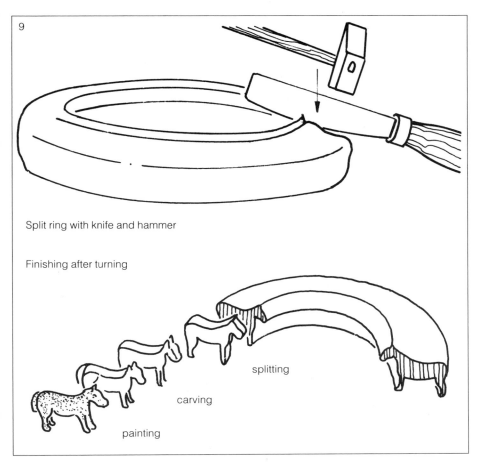

Split ring with knife and hammer

Finishing after turning

splitting

carving

painting

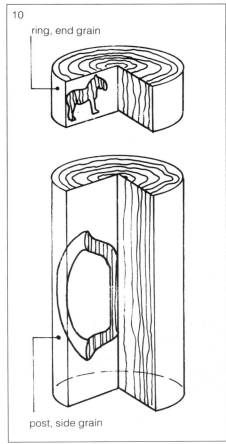

ring, end grain

post, side grain

The upright run of the grain allows the turned ring to be easily split into many parts after turning.
The rough disc is mounted on a cup chuck and turned completely round with a gouge.
The face of the wood is levelled with a skew chisel.

Using specially shaped tools (Fig 11), the disc is turned into a ring with the contours of an animal.
Two working processes with many individual phases are necessary to shape the contours of a horse. In the first process the underside is formed, i.e. the belly, fore and hind legs and the under-part of the head. The ring is now turned around and mounted on a suitably large spigot chuck to turn the upper side, consisting of the head, neck and back. Depending on the quality of the animal in the ring, up to 15 different turning tools may be required.
The contours of the animal cannot be seen properly until the ring is divided into small pieces with a knife and a hammer. Afterwards the final shape is achieved by additional carving and perhaps painting.
Up to 60 animals can be produced out of a ring of about 40 cm diameter.

A special feature of ring-turning is that the wood is wet when turned, in contrast to the usual procedure. Wet wood, e.g. lime, alder, birch or fir, is soft and easy to work. Before it has had time to dry and form cracks it has already been cut into small pieces which, because of their size, will no longer split.

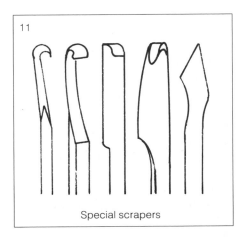

Special scrapers

The spire for a historic wooden model (Fig 2) is being turned in Figs 1-11. When it has been roughed down to a cylinder the blank is screwed to a chuck with a spacing disc.

The use of the spacing disc is important as it prevents the tools from touching the faceplate of the screw chuck.
A gouge is used to turn the blank to its approximate shape and size.

The workpiece is then turned to a cone shape with a skew chisel, working from the base to the point (Fig 10). When working towards the point, tool pressure must be decreased. The length of the cone must be well worked out beforehand.

Spires and domes may also be assembled out of different elements. The assembly of spires and domes shown in Fig 12 is reminiscent of a colourful crowd of people.

10

11

12

Making skipping-rope handles is an easy task for the amateur turner, and does not take up too much time.
In our example two handles are turned from one pinewood blank.

When the markings have been made (Fig 1) the handles are given a manageable ogee shape with a skew chisel (see Figs 3, 4, 8). The ends are beaded using a gouge (Fig 2).

When they have been smoothed and sanded (Fig 6) the handles are cut apart in a mitre box, using a tenon saw (Fig 9).

The hole for the rope is bored vertically through the handles using a twist drill. If the bit is too short to go all the way through, the handle is turned around and bored from the opposite end.
It is recommended that you leave a slightly larger hollow for the knot to fit into. The skipping rope should be 1.5 m long.

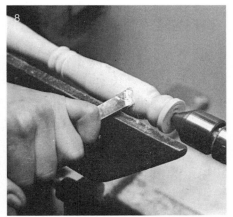

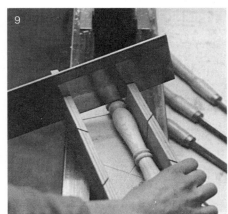

The climbing frame (Fig 10) is made up of rods; knots in the rope keep the rods apart.
The swing (Fig 12) consists of rods and coloured beads strung together above a wooden seat.

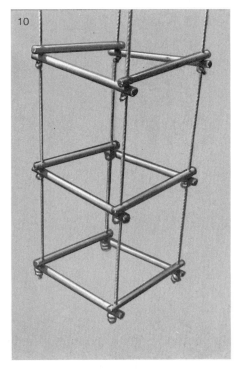

Profiled bars are common to stools, chairs and tables, and on these are mainly in the form of spindle-turned profiles and ends. According to taste at the time, the profiles either change or are repeated in a modified form.

Stools are usually constructed coarsely. They do not have much profile, but the little they do have stands out all the more. The height of the seats is extremely variable; one only has to think of children's high chairs or of bar stools. They can have either three or four legs, although some exceptions have turned, central columns.

Chairs display many varieties of turning in their backs and arms, in spindles and stretchers, as well as in their legs and feet. Antique chairs are more richly profiled than modern ones, but even these last have some profiling.

Only occasionally do beds and couches have turned posts and spindles. Cradles, particularly antique models, are lovingly decorated with turned wooden parts.

Tables, either on a central column or with vertical or sloping legs, often have interesting profiles and details. Furniture framework with additional parts of the same or of a different kind creates a very modern design.

Experimentation in this area may cause strong feelings, but antique models may well be the inspiration behind such work.

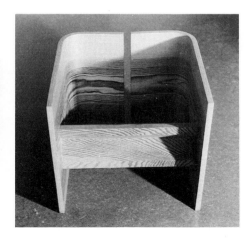

Bar profiles appear in all turned furniture work. Table and chair legs, bed and cupboard posts, all have similar profiles.

To avoide repetition on the following pages, common features are shown here and more details are given later in the appropriate sections.
The basic models and runs of similar or different profiles are shown here.

1 Basic profiles

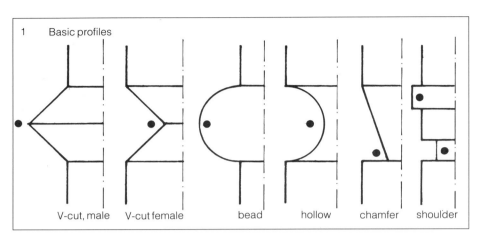

V-cut, male V-cut female bead hollow chamfer shoulder

2 Ogees

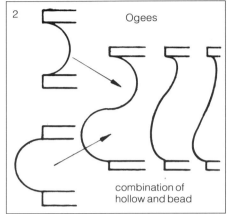

combination of hollow and bead

3 runs of the same profile profiles

extended

Interrupted runs of the same profile

4

5 cupboard post

bed post

chair leg

table leg

Use of bars

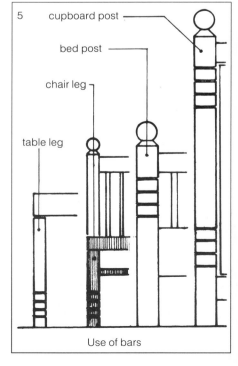

6

profiles, accents

partial complete partial

7

The upper and lower bar ends, those at the top and the foot of the bars, can be divided into two main groups. Endings turned with the bar can be produced economically as they produce little wastage.

Profiles which are produced separately and mounted later may well be wider than the bars, in which case they also cause very little wastage.

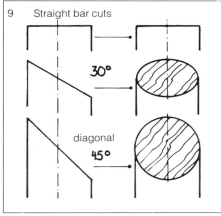

Straight bar cuts

30°

diagonal

45°

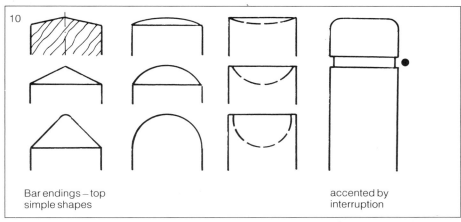

Bar endings – top simple shapes

accented by interruption

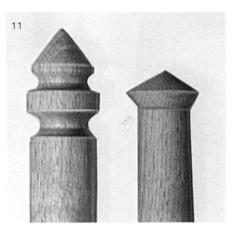

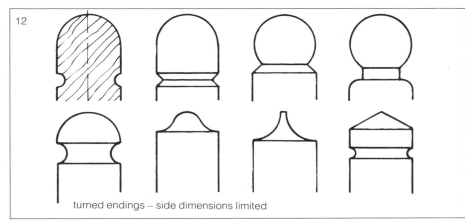

turned endings – side dimensions limited

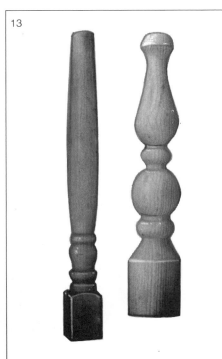

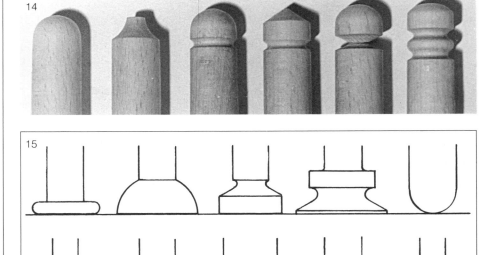

Bar endings – foot

There are a tremendous variety of
stools. They are almost always made
of turned work, even if they do not
always have profiling.

The shapes of the seats range from
circular and semi-circular forms to
squares with well-rounded corners.
The design of stools is usually plain
and simple. Even so, legs and
stretchers are very finely turned.
Richly profiled legs (see Fig 5) appear
thick-set and compact.

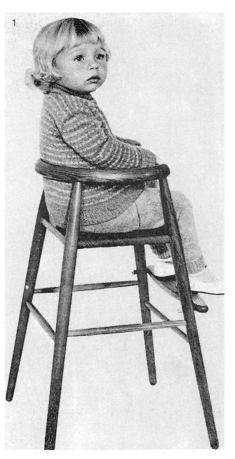

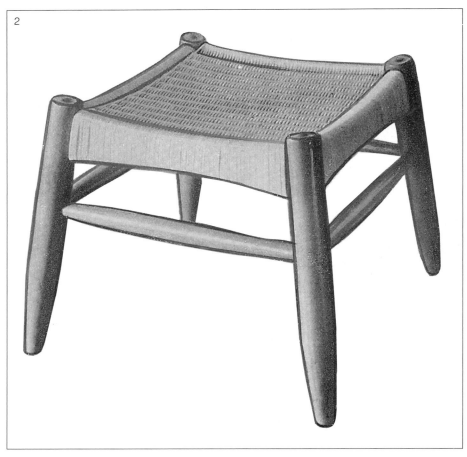

Compared to chair seats, stool seats
are often extremely high or low.
High chairs which enable children to
sit at tables constructed for adults are
above average height, as are bar
stools.

On the other hand, normal-sized
children's stools, footstools, folding
stools and milking stools must be very
low. A stool may have either a central
column, three legs (which prevents it
from wobbling), or four legs (so that it
cannot be tipped easily).

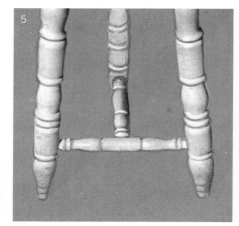

6

7

8

The legs may be fixed in a vertical or slanting position. Folding stools are the exception, as they have horizontal bars at ground level.

To assemble a stool, the legs are jammed into the underside of the seat and then secured with seat rails and stretchers of various numbers and in various positions.

9

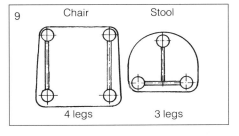

10

11

12

177

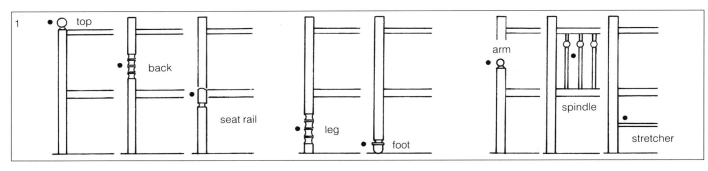

1

top
back
seat rail
leg
foot
arm
spindle
stretcher

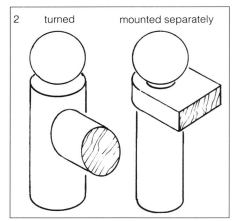

2

turned   mounted separately

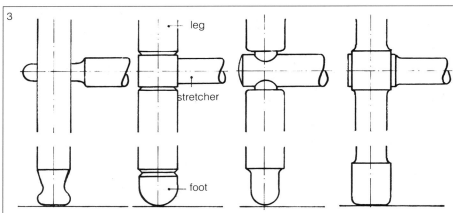

3

leg
stretcher
foot

The knob on the arm, which may either be turned with the leg or mounted afterwards has always been an area for new designs.

The transition from a right-angled to a round profile creates tapering forms which are not unattractive.

The simple, sailcloth chair in Fig 6 is designed in this individual, convincing way.

Turned chair-legs are mounted separately in the seat-rails of chairs made with solid wooden seats, or, when stretchers are used, they are set into bored holes.

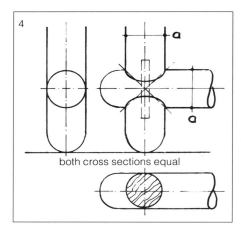

4

a

a

both cross sections equal

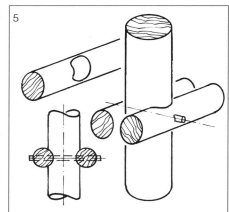

5

6

7

8

There are numerous possibilities for incorporating turned work in chairs. The ways in which the members are joined together for technical reasons can often show effective variations. The fitting together of bars of similar or different thicknesses, in pairs or in combined forms has always been a problem that has sought and found contemporary solutions.

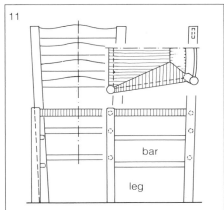

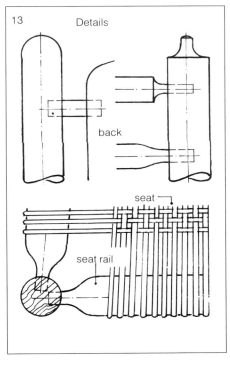

The joints of the bars may be made abruptly from the wood of one thickness to that of another, or they may lead together smoothly.
In any case the bars should be at right angles to the bore hole (see Fig 13). Alternatively, the bore hole can be conical as in Fig 14.

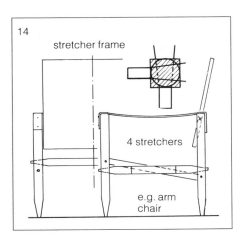

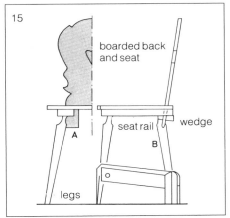

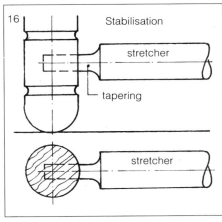

Antique chairs, depending on when they were made, have particularly rich profiles.

The design of certain individual chairs can even today be described as 'good to excellent'.

The bars and their upper and lower ends present balanced proportions and harmony. These antique chairs set an example for today's designer, which is the reason for showing them here. This is not intended as an invitation to copy them, however.

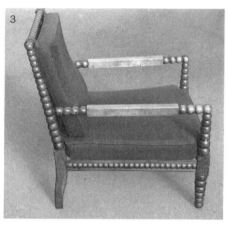

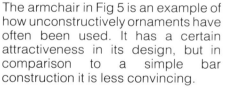

The armchair in Fig 5 is an example of how unconstructively ornaments have often been used. It has a certain attractiveness in its design, but in comparison to a simple bar construction it is less convincing.

The example of a very daring chair-back construction is Fig 2 shows how nonchalantly individual motifs were sometimes put together.

8

9

10

Compared to past ages, the time we live in is not influenced so much by harmony as by contrast.

New shapes which are created will not be able to be seen as typical of our time as emphatically as antique furniture is.

The joining of the crossed stretchers in Fig 9 illustrates one way in which the central point of turned bars may be formed. The joining of the individual bars in a square is excellent both technically and functionally. The knob above the square gives an artistic emphasis to the design of the joint.

11

12

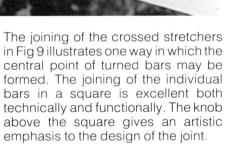

13

knob

spindle

seat rail

stretcher

leg

Beds, cradles and bedside tables often have a lot of turned work on their feet, legs and spindles.

Antique examples of this are superior to the modern ones in their richness and beauty. It would have been an easy task to fill two pages of this book with such examples. However, the aim of this book is, as well as to show the technical details of woodturning, to stimulate the reader into producing designs suitable for today.

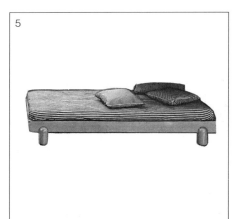

The modern examples (Figs 10 and 11) do not have much profiling, but they are just as typical of the present day as the antique examples were in their own time, and of as high a quality.

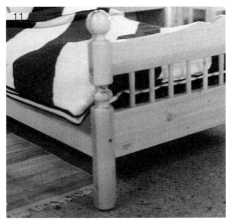

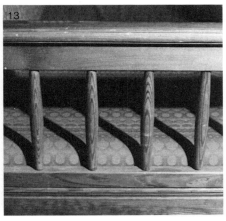

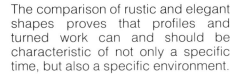

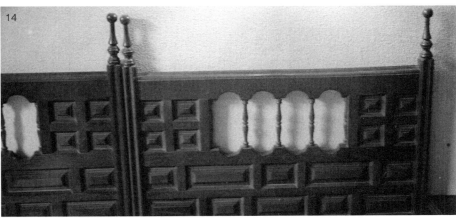

The comparison of rustic and elegant shapes proves that profiles and turned work can and should be characteristic of not only a specific time, but also a specific environment.

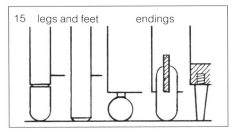

15 legs and feet   endings

16

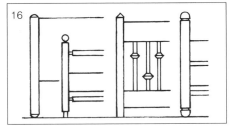

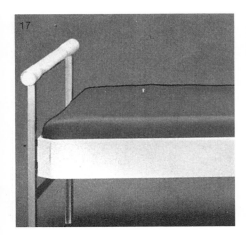

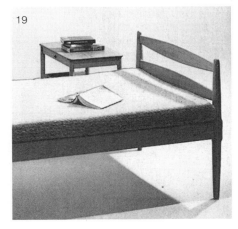

Tables present many interesting details, particularly where turning is concerned. The cross-sections and shapes of the legs – circle, half-circle and quarter-circle – afford many creative possibilities: contours running parallel to each other or tapering, positioned vertically or at a more sloping angle.

The ends of the legs are just as highly expressive as the top and frame joints. The abstract, diagrammatic comparisons and practical examples on the following pages show how much the basic possibilities for giving distinctive characteristics to the individual pieces have been used and developed.

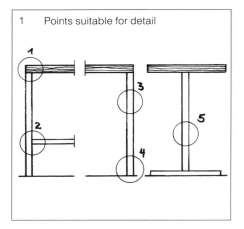

1   Points suitable for detail

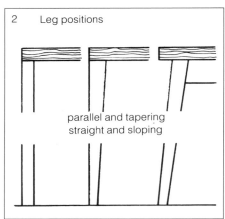

2   Leg positions

parallel and tapering
straight and sloping

3

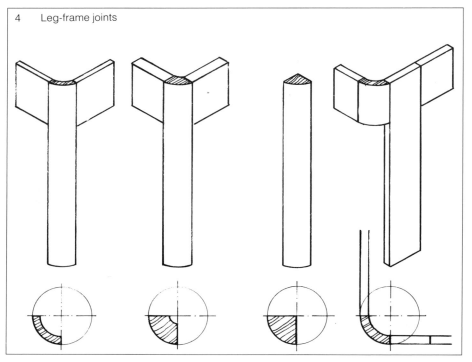

4   Leg-frame joints

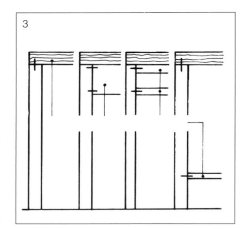

5   Positioning (table from below)

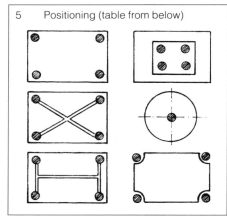

6   Cross sections   (3)

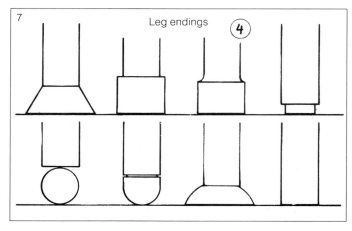

7   Leg endings   (4)

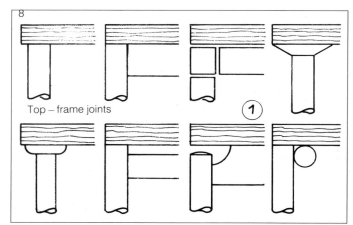

8

Top – frame joints   (1)

184

The frame joints in Fig 9 have been restricted to dowels as these can be bored and so suit turned work better than do timber joints.

There are many varieties of dowel joint which are interesting from the point of view of design.

The addition of similar or dissimilar parts to the framework allows further interesting creations, e.g. the combination of bars and boards at particular angles or the use of wooden balls for strengthening or joining (Fig 10 and 11).

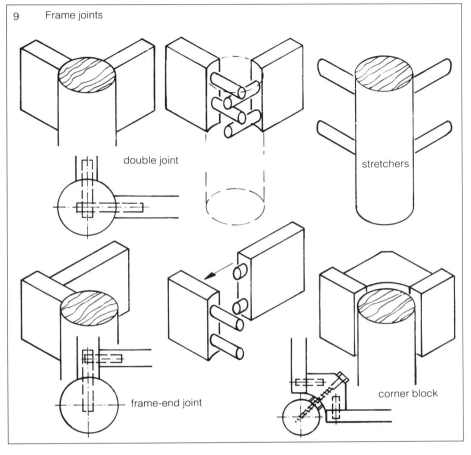

9   Frame joints

double joint

stretchers

frame-end joint

corner block

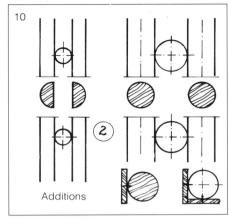

10

Additions

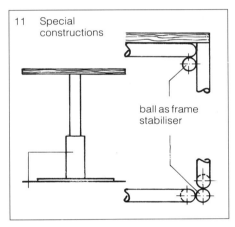

11   Special constructions

ball as frame stabiliser

Figs 13 and 14 show the top of a drawing table, which is adjustable by means of a turned shaft equipped with adjustment pegs.

Central columns are very common on round tables. They may be suported by a varied number of legs or stands on a base, which may be richly profiled, quite smooth or even flat.

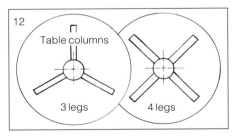

12   Table columns

3 legs

4 legs

13

14

15

Collapsible tables have removable legs. This means they are less bulky to transport, easier to pack and easily reassembled. Using wooden or metal threads, the legs are screwed either directly into the table-top, into a reinforcing block or into the frame.

The patented AMCO universal table-frame is excellent for screwing on table legs, even at an angle. This is ideal for both the amateur and the professional turner.
Thus released from the technical difficulties of table-construction, turners can now concentrate fully on profiling the table legs.

Slots cut in table frames mean that the blocks which support the table top can be mounted flexibly. Thus even tops made of solid wood which might warp, as well as of cross-veneered wood, can be fixed flush to the frame.

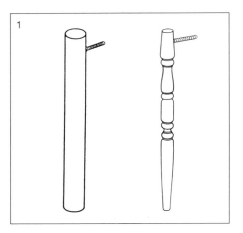

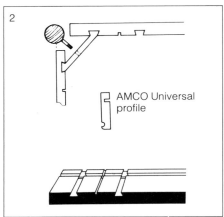

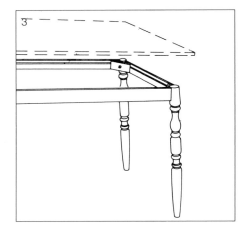

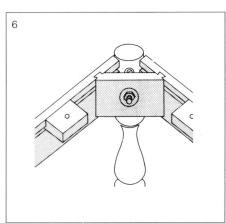

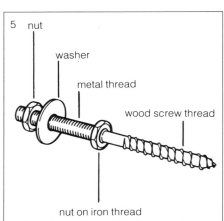

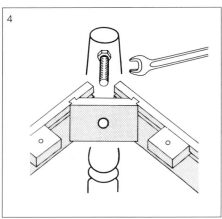

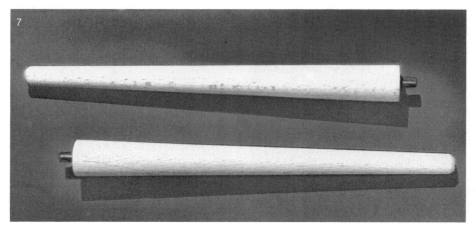

Antique tables sometimes combine very rich profiling with large projections. The bulky parts of the table legs in Fig 10 were certainly widened by gluing on blocks before they were turned.

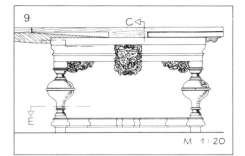

9

C◁

M 1:20

10

11

The central column of the table in Fig 13 has a projection half-way up. It must have been produced in one of two ways. In one method the wood is widened as described above, in the other the central column is cut into two pieces and the wide piece clamped like a plate between them. The parts of the column are joined by a dowel or a screw which goes right through the additional disc.

The table leg in Fig 11 was decorated with carved fluting after turning.
The table in Fig 14 was given additional feet beneath its cross base.

12

13

14

Although modern tables have hardly any profiled turning, they are often given round legs and columns. The positioning of the legs plays an important part in design, the problem being not whether to set them vertically or at an angle, but rather whether to use single legs or combinations.

It is popular to exaggerate the construction of table-top joints and the bases of central columns. New designs are partly a result of this strategy of exaggeration. We often find legs, bases or table-tops which are either unusually thick or unusually slender. This causes surprise and perplexity; in any case it has an effect – which is what it is all about.

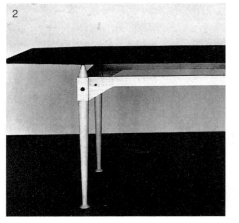

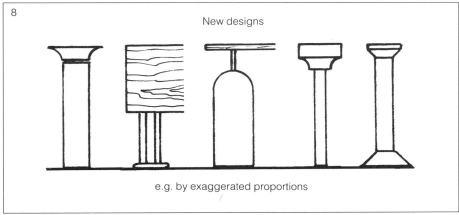

New designs

e.g. by exaggerated proportions

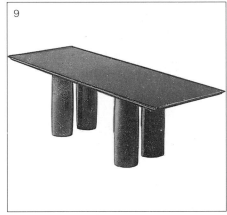

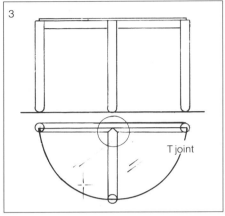

1

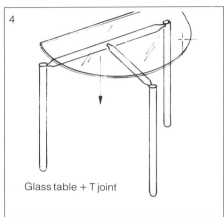

2

Figs 1 and 2 show the technical solution to the problem of joining two bars to make a T-shape, using a socket-head screw. The joint is functional and prototypes have proved its stability. The flush joint fits perfectly, but it kills the design. It offers nothing to attract the eye. We were therefore concerned with making a well-designed joint for such a problematic position.

3

T joint

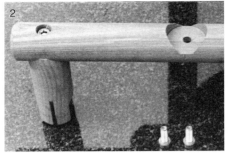

4

Glass table + T joint

5

T-joint, conventional,
not very stable

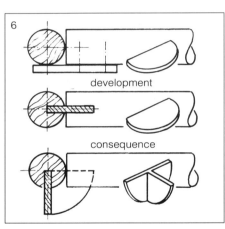

6

development

consequence

7

semicircular disc, screwed
from below

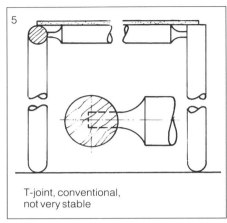

8

dowel

2 quarter circle
discs, dowelled

A semi-circular, glass-topped table with three legs and a T-shaped frame was the result of efforts to demonstrate modern table design using turned work (see Figs 3 and 4).

The remaining task was to find the constructive solution for the suggested T-shape.
The conventional method of joining bars (Fig 5) was rejected as unstable and too conventional (not modern enough).

Slotting or screwing in semi-curcular discs (see Figs 6 and 7) was accepted as progressive and suitable for the object in mind. However, the way the two bars were joined was still unacceptable. Figs 9-11 show further stages in the development of the joint using circular discs and rings.

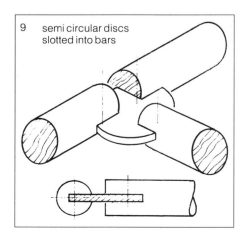

9   semi circular discs
    slotted into bars

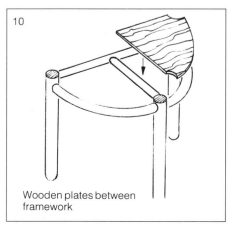

10

Wooden plates between
framework

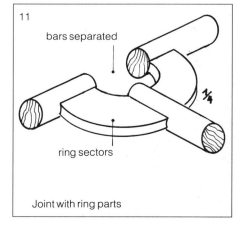

11   bars separated

ring sectors

Joint with ring parts

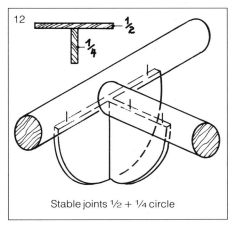

12

1/2
1/4

Stable joints 1/2 + 1/4 circle

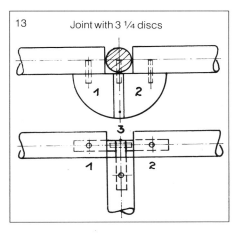

13 Joint with 3 1/4 discs

1 2

3

1 2

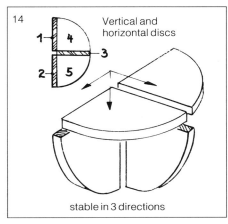

14 Vertical and horizontal discs

1 4
3
2 5

stable in 3 directions

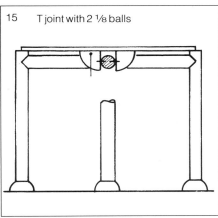

15 T joint with 2 1/8 balls

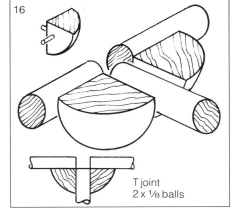

16

T joint
2 x 1/8 balls

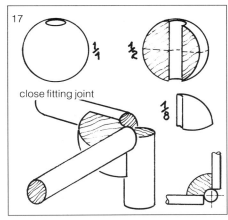

17

1/1 1/2

close fitting joint

1/8

The spatial development of the joints began with the addition of half and quarter-circles (see Fig 12).

Further experiment amounted to the combination of three quarter-circles (Fig 13) and led to the vertical and horizontal use of altogether five quarter-circle discs (drawn in Fig 14 and shown in Fig 18 as a model with six quarter-circle discs).

The result of attempts to find a three-dimensional construction was the use of sections of a wooden ball (Figs 15 and 16). The further development to a joint in the framework with the additional joint of a downward bar, shown in Fig 17.

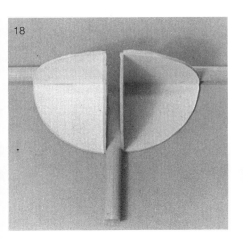

18

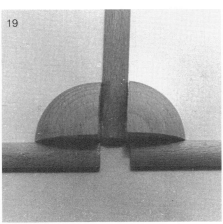

19

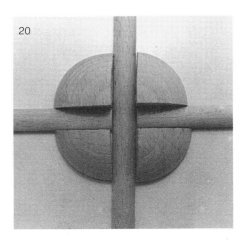

20

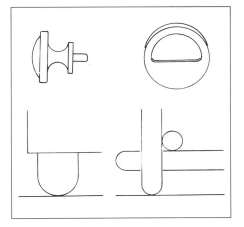

Depending on the type of furniture and its size, knobs for drawers and doors are made with very different sizes, contours and surfaces.

There are soft as well as hard forms, shapes constructed of one and of many parts. Antique knobs and finials decorate all sorts of objects. They are almost unique in the quality of their design.

Ornamental knobs on door panels are sometimes underlaid with rosettes, which add to their effect. Door pulls are found on sliding doors. They are first turned and then fitted into bore holes.

The corners of door frames are often made out of rings which have been cut and worked in between the straight parts of the frame.

Half-columns decorate furniture fronts, covering the sides of cupboards or the edges of double doors.

Feet made of turned wood – antique furniture, chairs, chests of drawers and cupboards are inconceivable without them – are finding a new function on modern furniture.

Turned frames beneath chests of drawers are rare – but perhaps tomorrow's possibilities are already presenting themselves today.

One of the first stages in turning a knob is to hammer in a blank (Fig 2).

The cylinder must first be roughed down to the correct diameter with a gouge.

The details will be cut later (continued on the following page).

A knob for a piece of furniture is to be turned from a pinewood blank.
The cylindrical blank must first be tapered slightly at one end to fit into the cup chuck (Fig 5).

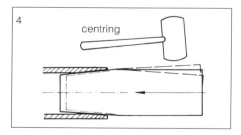

The blank is tapped into the cup chuck with a club hammer (Fig 4). It must fit tightly and be on centre.
The cylinder is first roughed with a gouge to the diameter required for the knob, and then the details are carefully turned. Caution and not too much pressure are called for.

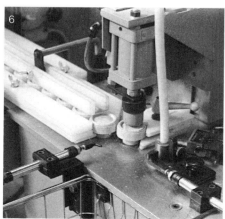

4
centring

A knob-turning machine is shown here (Fig 6) as a contrast to working by hand. Fig 10 shows that copy-turning is also possible to a certain extent on a normal lathe.

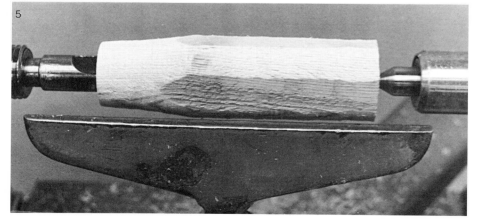

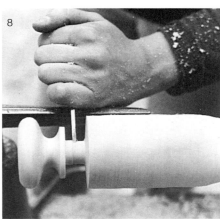

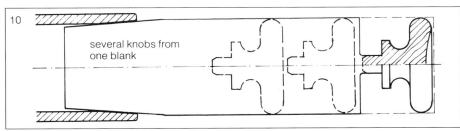

several knobs from
one blank

A dowel of 8-10 cm diameter for fixing the knob to a door or drawer is turned with it. The shape of the knob should be pleasant and smooth. Pointed or hard-edged shapes should be avoided.

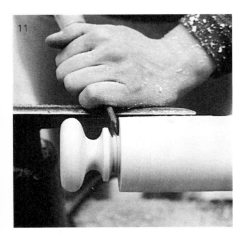

Antique knobs and finials have a charming gracefulness of shape. We find them as ornamentation on furniture such as chairs or clocks and on equipment such as spinning-wheels, swifts and tools.

The wealth of old turned work is fascinating; the variations are tremendous. Attractive and distinctive, the examples here witness to the carefree imagination of the craftsmen of old.

The surface finish ranged from oiling, varnishing and polishing the natural wood to applying coats of paint. The clock in Fig 2 is painted white and set off with gold; the clock in Figs 7 to 9 is stained black and polished.

The joining of crossed stretchers of a stool is not an easy problem to solve, as both bars should really be continuous. The development of a junction where four equal-sized bars meet is extremely rational. The additional design appears very skilful.

Fig 11: This old pressing board deserves our attention because of its subtle decoration. The board itself is shaped slightly conically and chamferred; the handle is fitted asymmetrically and has been finely turned. Even the part of the handle that is actually held by the hand is not the same on the right as on the left.

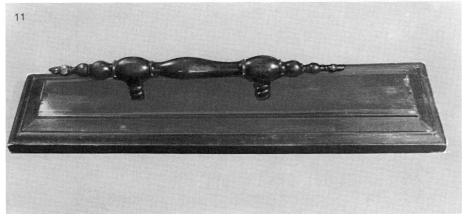

It is popular to leave the wood of knobs that are used to open and close drawers and doors of furniture in its natural state, as any surface treatment becomes worn away with time.

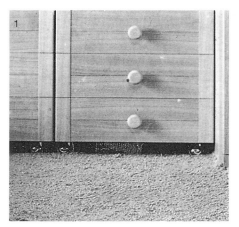

In principle the shape of a knob should be designed so that it can be gripped easily. Nevertheless, all kinds of knobs are to be found, particularly on small, light drawers. Alongside the usual rounded shapes it is also possible to find hard-edged knobs.

Knob sections are popularly formed according to the designer's taste; they may be everyday or highly individual, occasionally inset or turned in two parts (see Fig 2).

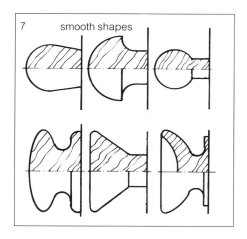

smooth shapes

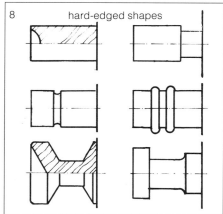

hard-edged shapes

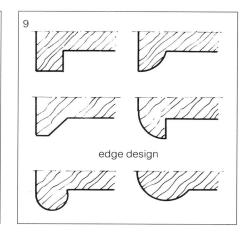

edge design

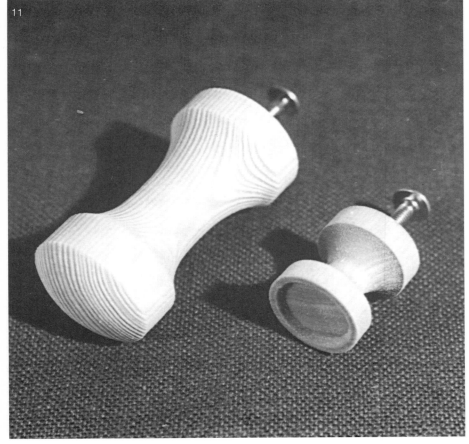

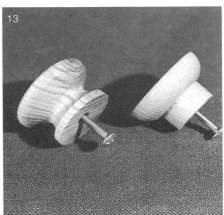

Knobs are always fixed in a concealed way, the easiest methods being to use a dowel that is turned with the knob, to use a separate dowel or to use a thread cut into the spigot left after turning (Fig 15). Fixing the knobs from behind is very practical and is done using screws or bolts.

Divided knobs are to be understood as such: a knob is divided into two parts which are fixed next to each other at the edges of two doors, so that each door can be opened separately, although the knobs form a single unit when the doors are closed.

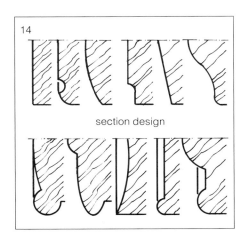

section design

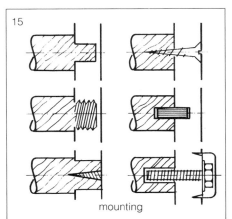

mounting

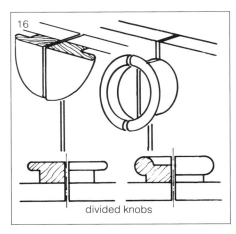

divided knobs

Door and drawer pulls are either turned into the solid piece of furniture, such as the front of a drawer, or they are worked separately and then mounted into a bore hole. The insides of the pulls must be undercut to counteract the strain which occurs when doors and drawers are opened. In the case of sliding doors, the pulls may be completely smooth inside.

Combinations of pulls and knobs often have a practical use, but may also serve as pure decoration.
The cupboard in Fig 2, for example, has knobs in the middle of the panels of high, framed doors.
The large knob is connected from behind to a flat, profiled disc by a metal screw which holds the wide door pull pressed firmly into position.

Figs 5-8 show pulls with knobs in one and more parts. They are either mounted from the front or pushed through from behind. It is better to conceal the bore holes by over-lapping them with the pull edges. The pulls also fit best when they project slightly. This is the only really neat and flush-fitting method.

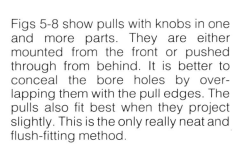

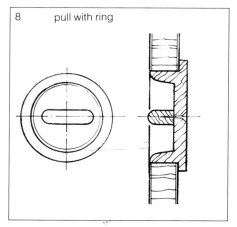

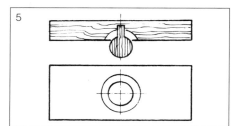
6   3-part drawer pull

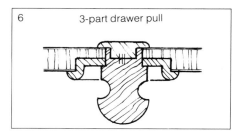

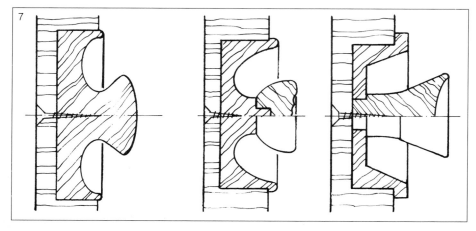
8   pull with ring

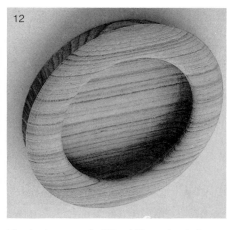

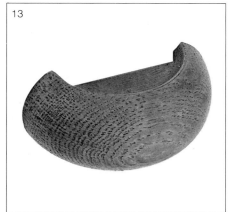

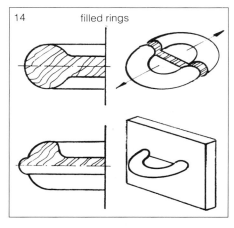

filled rings

Keyhole guards (Fig 15) protect doors from being damaged when keys are put into the keyholes.

Rings, either open or with a central disc (Fig 14), make good handles for doors, drawers or hinged lids when they are cut in half and mounted at right-angles to the surface.

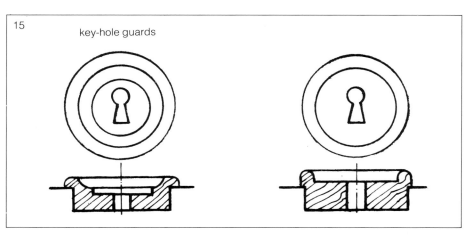

key-hole guards

The designing of rounded frame corners and parts of doors is an act of creation. The design is put into practice using turned rings from which the required pieces are cut.

Depending on what is needed, the frame corners are set either convexly or concavely. The same profiling can be used as the straight pieces of the frame, but the mitre of the profiled strip of wood must be filed to fit.
It is easier to cut a straight mitre, as profiling must always be fitted to the diagonal joint.

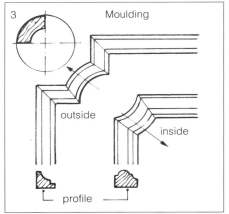

The edges of furniture are often turned, but nowadays they can also be moulded. Rounded edges of turned ring sections may be positioned horizontally or vertically, arching outwards or inwards. In all events, the joints between curved edges and straight parts must be stable.

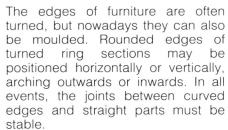

The corners of the window frames of the door in Figs 8 and 9 have been made from sections cut from turned wooden discs. When the strips of wood to hold the glass in position have been glued on, they are mitred on both sides of the door (Fig 10).

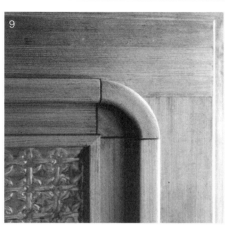

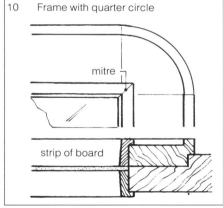

10   Frame with quarter circle

mitre

strip of board

The quarter-circle in Fig 14, also used in a door, serves additionally to support the pane of glass, in contrast to the disc in Fig. 10.

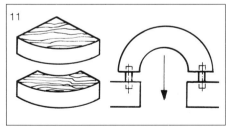

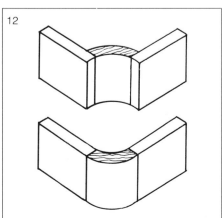

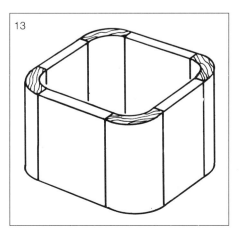

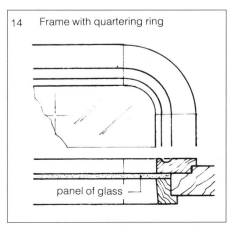

14   Frame with quartering ring

panel of glass

1

2

3

4

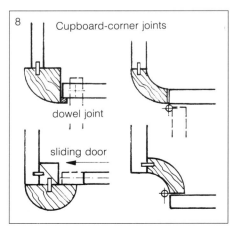

5

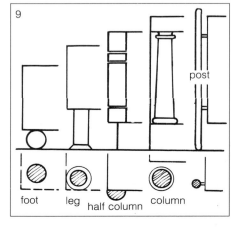

6

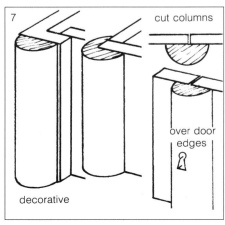

7

cut columns

over door
edges

decorative

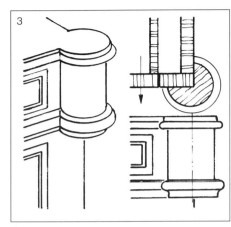

8

Cupboard-corner joints

dowel joint

sliding door

9

post

foot   leg   half column   column

204

Columns, whether round, halved or quartered, were once very popular furniture decoration. They were used as corner posts, to conceal joints between panels or as overlapping edges on double doors.

Columns used as plant stands or as cupboard decorations were very often carved after turning.
The cupboard in Fig 11 has been given a gallery-like balustrade similar to that on an old house.

Turned spindles in place of or inside door panels have become rare, but for this reason they are particularly interesting. In Germany they were once used on bread cupboards for ventilation purposes.

Furniture feet made of turned wood have always been popular. End grain wood can support very heavy weights without difficulty. The photographs on this page illustrate the turning of a short foot of beechwood. When the blank has been roughed, one end is rounded and the whole piece is sanded.

Beech is the most economical hardwood. Unlike oak it has very small pores and is good for staining or dyeing in all colours.
Depending on the growth and cut of the wood, pine has a conspicuous grain that is emphasised by turning.

The feet are generally mounted using dowelled joints. The dowel is either turned with the foot or fixed into a bore hole later.
Two dowels staggered against each other are better than one, as they prevent the foot being twisted off.

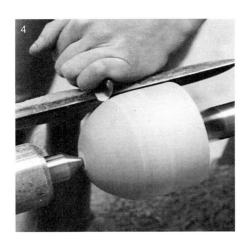

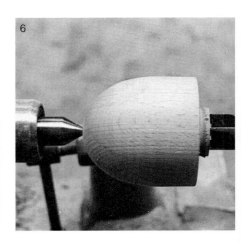

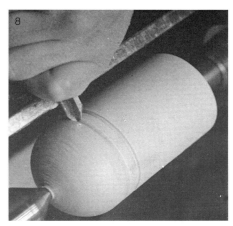

Fig 10 shows plain, simple furniture feet: cylinder, cone and ball.

Fig 11 shows the type of foot that is considered modern at present, rounded at one or both ends. The feet are either connected directly to the furniture or with a short space between.

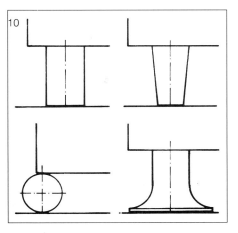

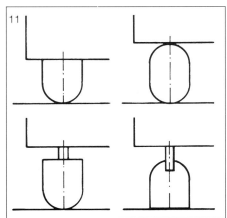

The feet of antique furniture were once very richly profiled, something which we are beginning to acknowledge again today.

Cupboard feet were short and wide, sometimes almost flat. Cutting a groove or a ridge around the widest part was popular, and emphasised the roundness.

The joint between foot and cupboard either occurs too abruptly, as in the cupboard in Fig 5, or it is emphasised by a fine transition, as in the foot of the chest of drawers in Fig 3.

Chair legs and the feet of easy chairs (Figs 1 and 2) are, by their function, much higher than cupboard feet, and therefore also more slender. The feet are either fitted beneath the chair frame or turned on the end of a chair leg.

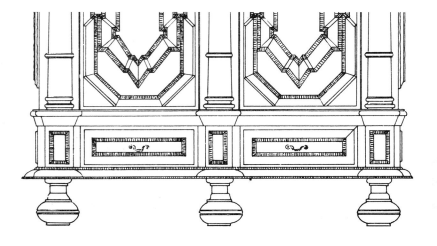

Feet are again being produced on modern furniture. Ball or sphere form is popular, as it is neutral and matches even the most unusual shapes.

Fig 6: It is the colouring rather than the profiling that distinguishes the ball feet of this writing desk with a triangular corpus and lectern-like attachment.

The model chest of drawers in Fig 7 has one foot shaped like a 'pencil' column. This detail was borrowed from the latest developments in building construction, a method always popular in furniture design.

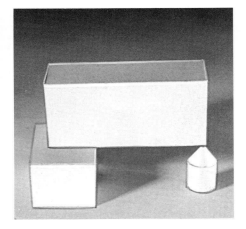

Fig 8: The wooden foot at the end of a tubular steel table leg can be explained by another planning strategy. The exaggeration of buildings or furniture parts characterises the contribution made by modern architecture.

The table in Fig 8 is exaggeratedly different, i.e. its legs are much too slender in comparison to the table top and feet.

The time in which we live demands design, but ornamentation is still dead, and even profiling is not really adequate. So a way has been found of improving simple features by exaggeration.

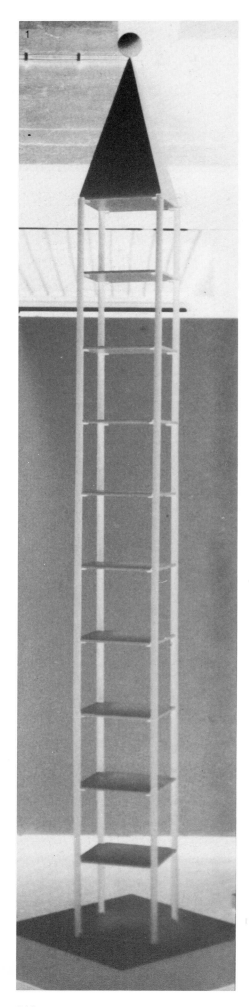

The construction of shelves does not present many possibilities for putting turning to use and so it shows up all the more on the few occasions when it is used. Wooden balls and circular discs set accents.

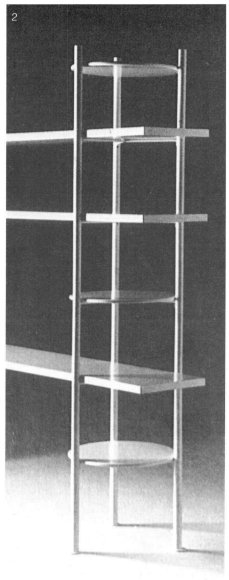

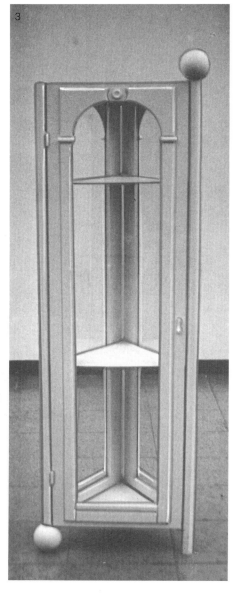

The legs of the cupboard frames shown here have all been turned. A comparison of the individual frames shows clearly how much change of effect can be achieved merely by tapering or thickening the legs a little. The frames are situated below the body of the cupboard to connect the legs.

In contrast, the stretchers can be freely arranged either lengthways or crosswise. Supports are sometimes used for additional stability.

Trolleys require additional stability, particularly as they are moved around. This problem is solved to advantage in the trolleys in Fig 11, in the shape of shelves.
The set of shelves in Fig 12 is easily dismantled and reassembled. The bars between the shelves are made of turned wood.

1

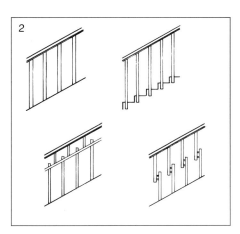

Banisters are still made out of turned wood. The design involves not only the profiling of the spindles, but also the way in which they are arranged. The distance between spindles, although it should not exceed a maximum of 12 cm, allows many different possible combinations.

New, experimental designs can be created by deliberately cutting and replacing the spindles (Fig 2).

Newel posts are today constructed in parts. Continuous newel posts have become very unusual. The ends of posts are still topped with knobs or finials.

Door-panels and door-frames are often decorated with wooden ornaments. Turned discs or halved columns are particularly suitable for this.

Balcony and veranda balusters turned from very stable wood are often still found in good condition on old buildings. It would be a challenge to re-introduce this tradition.

Wooden lattices are used as room-dividers, originally based on beautiful oriental models.

The use of woodturning for banisters has always been popular. The wood used should first be split: this is the only way to be sure that the run of the grain is straight and continuous. This is also the only way of guarding against breakage, even if the wood is hit at a right angle to the grain.

Design is always dependent on contemporary taste. Straightforward, slender spindles are favoured above richly profiled spindles, or vice versa. The range of possible shapes appears to be exhausted, however. It is exceedingly difficult to think up new variations.

Economic factors prohibit short, projecting forms, as too much wastage would occur in their production. The wood would have to be turned off almost the whole length of the spindle to produce one particularly wide section.

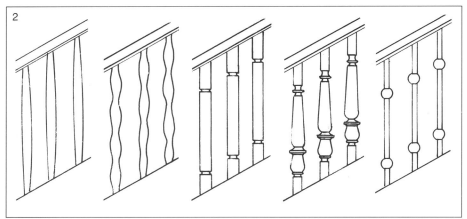

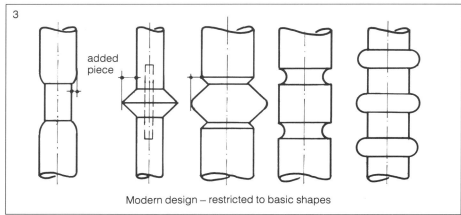
Modern design – restricted to basic shapes

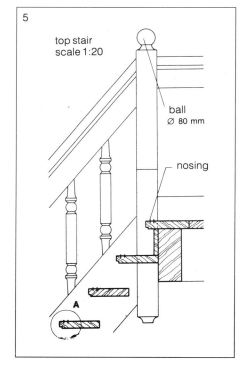
top stair
scale 1:20

ball
Ø 80 mm

nosing

A

214

Today, newels are generally set in parts between the steps. A steel bar is used to connect the individual sections firmly together.

Continuous newel posts on which the stairs are set are rare, since they cannot be made in advance and therefore prove expensive.

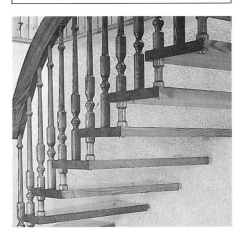

First banister posts are often set off with turned knobs or finials. The most suitable is a ball-shape, which fits nicely into the hand. Ball-shaped knobs are sometimes tilted, that is, have a slanting grain – which is only possible when the balls are turned separately.

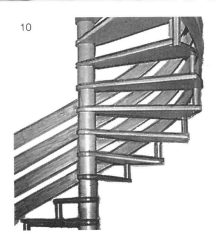

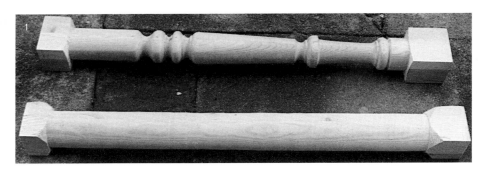

Banisters present a design not only in the contours of the individual spindles, but also in the way they are put together as a whole. For safety reasons the spindles should not be further than 12 cm apart, but within this limit they can be arranged in any way desired, at regular or irregular intervals. Cross connections divide the spindles horizontally and also give additional support.

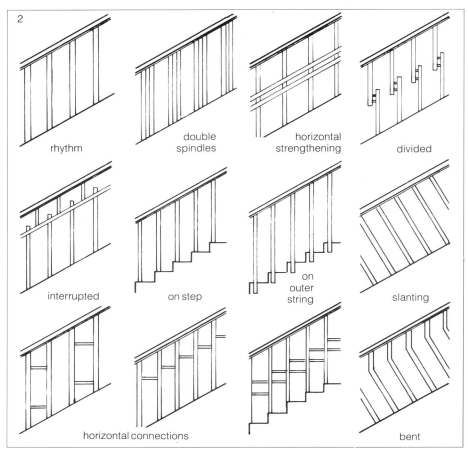

rhythm

double spindles

horizontal strengthening

divided

interrupted

on step

on outer string

slanting

horizontal connections

bent

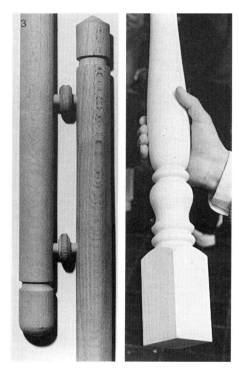

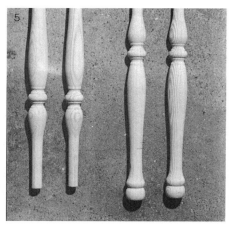

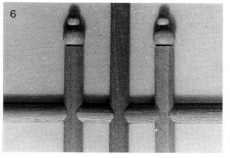

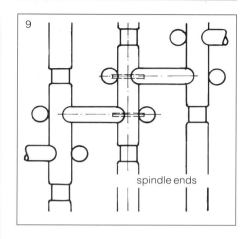

spindle ends

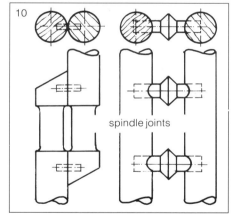

spindle joints

The desire to design a completely new shape of spindle gave rise to the series of models shown in Figs 11-17. The posts were deliberately cut and so ends appeared in places where they had never been seen before. The combinations are variable. Two or three pieces may be combined, either closely or spaced further apart.

Continuous spindles are also used, as are staggered parts.

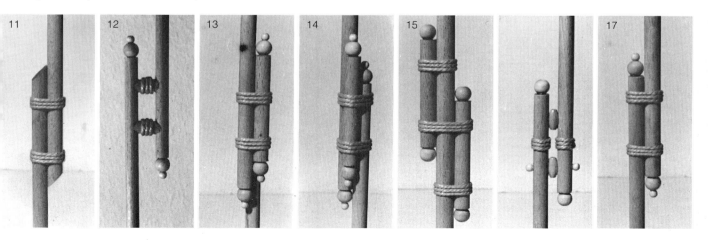

At first sight the most striking feature
of the gate shown in Figs 1 and 2 is the
row of wooden spikes. On closer
examination, the diagonal setting of
the partly squared bars stands out.
This gives the onlooker an additional
view.

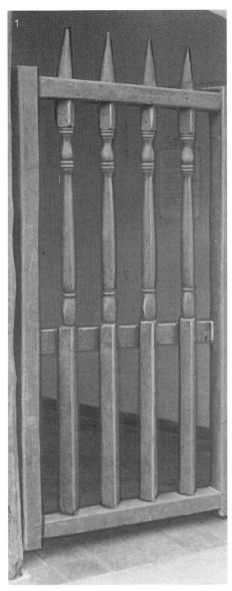

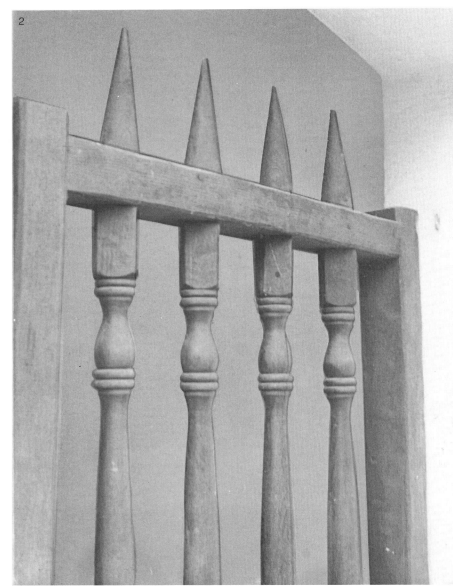

The design of doorways has not always been restricted to the door and its frame. The balustrade above the door in Fig 5 leads up to the balcony theme of pages 224-5. The ornate row of columns makes a conspicuous contrast to the sober door construction, with its diagonal brace.

balcony theme of pages 224-5

Fitments

Door grating

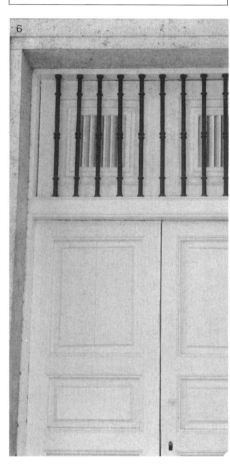

Wooden lattice-work is quite common in the Orient and in Latin America. In these areas it is mainly dry, even out of doors. In our climate, however, turned lattice-work must be restricted to use inside buildings, e.g. on room-dividers.

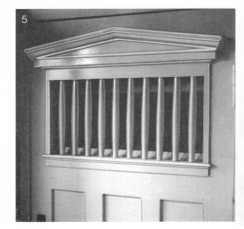

Columns, storey-high and thus quite thick, can be made waterproof by laminating plank-thick pieces of wood together. The inside should be left hollow to reduce tension.

Wood can be turned to decorate door panels or to make raised panels, as shown in Figs 1-11.

The size of raised panels is limited because of the possibility of the wood warping. The basic door construction may consist of a complete surface or of a framework. Raised panels are not usually glued to the door, but are rather screwed on from behind.

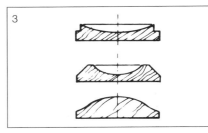

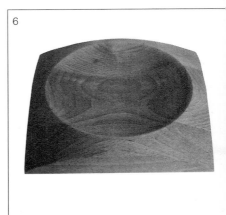

In frame constructions the panels are set in position from behind the framework and secured with strips of wood.

It used to be popular to ornately decorate both the framework and the panels.

The church door shown in Figs 7 and 8 has octagonal panels with strongly projecting turned centres.

The front-door panels in Figs 9-11 are all square. The transition from square to circle plays a particularly important part in the design.

Fitments

Door panels

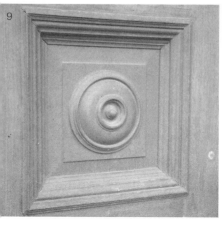

Fitments

Balcony balustrades

Stable, wooden balcony and veranda balustrades turned with strong profiling have become very scarce. Old balustrades are all the more conspicuous and make us aware of the failings of modern building.

The balusters were positioned in continuous rows or in groups, the posts being given particular emphasis from time to time.

The turned drops under the bay-window posts of Figs 5 and 6 illustrate the possible finishing touches that building components can be given.

The simple solution of just cutting off the wood at a right angle has become so natural to us that such light-hearted methods as this turned post can give great pleasure.

The time has come when we should return to designing our environment more individually. Turned building components could contribute to this.

The antique examples on these pages show that there are opportunities for creating designs and putting them to use. Simple safety barriers they may be, and so purely functional elements, but they were shaped with such intensity that history can be read from them.